# HOW
# TO
# WIN
# OTHERS
# TO
# CHRIST

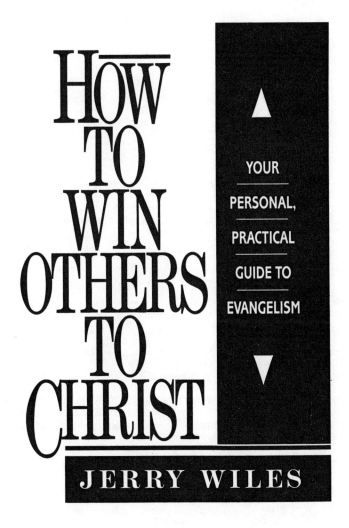

# HOW TO WIN OTHERS TO CHRIST

▲

YOUR

PERSONAL,

PRACTICAL

GUIDE TO

EVANGELISM

▼

JERRY WILES

OLIVER
NELSON

THOMAS NELSON PUBLISHERS
Nashville

Published in Nashville, Tennessee, by Oliver-Nelson Books, a division of
Thomas Nelson, Inc., Publishers, and distributed in Canada by Lawson
Falle, Ltd., Cambridge, Ontario.

Unless otherwise noted, the Bible version used in this publication is THE
NEW KING JAMES VERSION. Copyright © 1979, 1980, 1982, Thomas Nelson, Inc., Publishers.

Scripture quotation marked NIV is taken from the HOLY BIBLE: NEW IN-
TERNATIONAL VERSION. Copyright © 1973, 1978, 1984 by the International Bible Society. Used by permission of Zondervan Bible Publishers.

Scripture quotation noted AMPLIFIED BIBLE is from The Amplified Bible: Old
Testament, copyright © 1962, 1964 by Zondervan Publishing House (used by
permission) and from The Amplified New Testament, copyright © 1958 by
the Lockman Foundation (used by permission).

**Library of Congress Cataloging-in-Publication Data**

Wiles, Jerry, 1946–
    How to win others to Christ / Jerry Wiles.
        p.    cm.
    ISBN 0-8407-9621-8 (pbk.)
    1. Discipling (Christianity)   2. Witness bearing (Christianity)
I. Title.
BV4520.W485   1992
248'.5—dc20                                                              92-18659
                                                                             CIP

Printed in the United States of America.

1 2 3 4 5 6 — 97 96 95 94 93 92

To
My wife
*Sheila*
and to my children
*Jonathan* and *Sarah Beth*
and
In memory of some of God's choice servants
who influenced my life in the mid-1970s
and who have gone on to be with the Lord:

*Miss Bertha Smith*
*Dr. C. L. Culpepper*
*Evangelist Manley Beasley*
*Dr. Vance Havner*
*Dr. Alan Redpath*

I also want to acknowledge others who have had an impact
on my spiritual walk with the Lord and who have inspired
me to win others to Christ:

My parents
*Rev. and Mrs. Noble Wiles*

and

*Mr. Wayne Belt*
*Dr. Doug Hodo*
*Major Ian Thomas*
*Dr. Adrian Rogers*
*Dr. John A. Hash*

Finally, I wish to express my appreciation to
*Mrs. Roberta Hromas* and *Dr. Jan Dargatz*
for their involvement in helping this project
become a reality.

# CONTENTS

# THOSE WHO WIN SOULS ARE WISE

Personal evangelism is not a special gift given only to a few Christians. It is the responsibility of each one of us who follows the Lord Jesus. Jesus didn't put any qualifiers on His command: "You shall be witnesses to Me . . . to the end of the earth" (Acts 1:8).

God's plan is for all Christians to experience a life of fruitfulness—of seeing others come to Christ through their witness. In other words, God doesn't want any Christian to be denied the great *joy* of winning souls.

How do you overcome your reluctance to witness about the Lord? First, you must recognize the adequacy of Christ living in you rather than rely on your own abilities. You can trust Him to do the work of convicting a person's heart. You need only share news of Him and give others the opportunity to meet Him personally.

Second, you can acquire certain skills and insights that will help you face the challenge with eagerness and joy. This book will help you acquire those skills.

Above all, the purpose of this book is to free you to witness about Jesus and to win souls. It is not intended to burden you or to condemn you in any way. My greatest desire is to help you discover that

- it's easy to witness about Christ,
- it's natural—in fact, recognizing and pursuing opportunities to witness about Christ should become such a natural, normal part of every day that words about Jesus are

your first response to a question, crisis, or encounter, and,

- it's the most rewarding activity in which you can ever engage.

Jesus told His disciples to "pray the Lord of the harvest to send out laborers into His harvest" (Matthew 9:38). That is also my prayer for you!

—*Jerry Wiles*

*"By this we know that we abide in Him, and He in us, because He has given us of His Spirit. And we have seen and testify that the Father has sent the Son as Savior of the world. Whoever confesses that Jesus is the Son of God, God abides in him, and he in God."*

—1 John 4:13–15

# ONE

# DAILY ENCOUNTERS, ETERNAL DECISIONS

"It looks as if you've had a hard day, today," I said to the man seated next to me on the subway.

"Yeah, it was a pretty hard day," he responded.

I asked him a couple of other casual questions about what type of work he did and if he was on his way home. Then I asked, "Is there anything encouraging happening in your life?"

He said, "Nah. There's *nothing* encouraging happening in *my* life."

"Well, there are encouraging things happening in this city," I said. "I just met a woman who accepted Jesus Christ into her life, and she experienced great encouragement. In fact, she said that it was the most encouraging thing that had ever happened to her. I know that to be true in my life, too."

He said, "I'm a Muslim," and he named the African nation from which he had emigrated.

I said, "Well, a number of Muslims these days are finding that they need to be forgiven of their sins and that the only way to do that is to invite the Lord Jesus into their lives as their Savior. I spoke to a couple of Muslims just a few months ago who found a higher peace and reality in Jesus Christ."

He shrugged his shoulders and made no response. At the next stop, he got off.

As he got off the subway, I found myself facing the two young women who had been seated on the other side of him. One of them was smiling. I began to share with them, realizing they had overheard every word of my prior conversation. One of them said, "We're Catholic."

I said, "You know, a number of Catholics are finding a new relationship with the Lord Jesus these days. They are discovering that just going to church and going through the ritual of the liturgy isn't enough for them. They're seeking a more personal, intimate relationship with God, and they're finding a new spiritual life through inviting Jesus Christ to come into their lives in a personal way."

As I spoke with them, I noted that they were interested in what I was saying. They didn't turn away. They didn't raise objections. I asked, "You've been thinking about this already, haven't you?"

They both said, "Yes, I have been thinking about these things." We didn't have an opportunity to pray together since their stop was the next one, but over lunch, I began a very similar line of conversation with the waitress who served my table. She told me that she had been thinking more about spiritual matters lately and that she didn't really know what direction to take. I shared with her the fact that Jesus Christ was the source of all spiritual reality in my life and that what He had done for me, I was sure He would do for her. We prayed together so that she might receive Jesus into her life as her personal Savior, and I left her with a small piece of literature about how to grow in the Lord.

A new soul was added to the kingdom of heaven. A new name was written in glory. One out of four.

That's about an average response rate, at least, in my experience.

That day in Washington, D.C. I had the opportunity to bring two other people to the point of receiving Jesus Christ in their lives. In all, I had about fifteen conversations about the Lord, some of them with more than one person present. Not a great percentage if you're expecting an ideal 100 percent performance in life. And yet, life doesn't operate according to 100 percent performances. In the real world . . .

- Most retail shopkeepers would be thrilled if one out of every four people who came into their store made a purchase.

- Most salesmen would be extremely happy to have one in four clients place an order.
- Most baseball players would be very satisfied to get a hit every fourth time at bat—or perhaps more appropriate to the analogy, a "run batted in."

I did not focus on the people with whom I talked that day who did not receive Jesus as their personal Savior. In some cases, I know a seed of the gospel was planted in their lives. In other cases, I felt as if the Holy Spirit may have used my words to further the work He was doing in preparing their hearts for the Lord. In every case, I have confidence that I was doing what my Savior has commanded me and every other Christian to do—and for that, I will have a reward in heaven for obedience, regardless of the response of the other person.

Rather than think about those who didn't receive the Lord that day, I rejoice with heaven about those who did.

Three new souls with whom I can anticipate living forever in the presence of the Lord!

Three souls snatched from the clutches of the devil and the fate of hell!

Three souls starting a new walk with the Lord Jesus on the unending road of eternal life!

Three souls who can now experience the abundant joy and peace that come with knowing Jesus!

Three people won for Jesus. Friend, there's no greater joy!

## What Is Your Faith Level for Winning Souls?

Three souls in a day?
Five souls a month?
One soul a year?
What are you willing to believe God can do? That's probably your faith level today for seeing people come to the Lord.

Actually, there's nothing mystical or magical about bringing people to Christ in numbers large or small. It's simply a matter of talking to a lot of people and, in the course of those conversations, bringing up the name of Jesus.

In nearly twenty years now of active soul winning, I've found that there are two very important keys to bringing people to the Lord:

1. Know who you are in Christ and who He is in you.
2. Be willing to bring up the name of Jesus in a conversation.

## My Promise to You

As a born-again believer and follower of the Lord Jesus Christ, you have the authority to be His witness. Indeed, you are His witness. And His presence within you equips you for the task.

Therefore, speak boldly of Him. Your sharing the word of the Lord and the good news about what Jesus Christ did on the Cross is vital and valuable beyond price to this world. It's the very dew of spiritual life to water a dry and thirsty world and it will bring forth life.

Believe it! And "according to your faith let it be to you," says Jesus. (See Matthew 9:29.)

T W O

# GOD'S PART, YOUR PART

In its purest form, soul winning is putting yourself in a position for the Holy Spirit to win souls through what He prompts you to say and do.

If you see soul winning as something that you, in your own strength and ability, are *supposed* to do, then you will always feel burdened. You'll always feel inadequate. You'll always feel pressured. You'll always feel guilty for not doing more and frustrated that you can't do enough. On the other hand, if you see soul winning as letting Christ use you and work through you, then it's a joy to see what He will do next with your life!

## Doing for God versus God Doing Through Us

Many Christians have spoken of soul winning as something they are "doing for God."

The truth is that the Lord desires to use you as a part of the process of winning souls in order to do something in you and through you.

We are His instruments.

The wonderful thing about instruments is that they are tools in the hands of others. You are God's instrument to win souls. He directs and uses you. You yield. When I take a pen in my hand to write a letter, that pen becomes an instrument subject to my will and direction. You and I are God's instruments, used by Him to write living letters of His love to this world.

This awareness of who we are in Christ and who He is in us is at the core of our ability to win souls. It is not only the foundation, but the motivation, for what we do and say.

- If you don't know who you are in Christ, then how can you help others get to that point?
- If you don't know who Christ is in you, then what is it that you're offering somebody else?

# Who Are You?
# Who Is He?

Who am I in Christ?

Who is Christ in me?

Have you answered these two critically important questions in a definitive way in your own life?

Your ability to be a creative witness for the Lord is directly related to your having settled those key questions in your own life.

Before you can ever share with others who Christ can be in their lives, you must have an assurance of who He is in your life and who you are in Him.

First, you must acknowledge anew that He does, indeed, live within us.

Second, you must acknowledge anew that the Lord's presence in your life makes you complete. He has equipped you by His own life indwelling your life and has given you all things that pertain to life and godliness.

Who is the Jesus who lives in you? What is His nature? He is righteous. All-powerful. Holy. Forever victorious and strong. Loving. Wise.

All of these things are in direct contrast to what we are in our natural state. As human beings, apart from Christ we are unrighteous, unholy. We have little or no power and are rarely as loving or wise as we desire to be. Our victories are fleeting at best.

However, as Christ indwells you with His spirit, He endows you with His nature. You no longer need rely only on your own righteousness, your own strength, your own wisdom, and your own ability to love. You can rely on His righteousness, His strength, His wisdom, and His ability to love to flow *through* you.

He takes on who you are in order for you to become like Him. He was born of the Spirit of God and conceived of the Holy Spirit in order to do what He did. As Major Ian Thomas puts it:

> He had to come as He came . . . born of the Spirit of God and conceived of the Holy Spirit to be what He was . . . a demonstration of the glory and power of God
> to do what He did . . . die on the cross for the redemption of our lives
> that we might have what He is . . . LIFE
> to be what He was!—a present-day demonstration of the glory and power of God.

That's the gospel in a nutshell!

When Jesus Christ indwells you, He restores you to the full humanity that God intended for man when He first created him.

You become a representative of His nature. Your very life is a witness to the indwelling power of God.

# Witnessing Is Based on Something You Are

Many times we think of witnessing as something we do. We equate it with passing out tracts or ringing doorbells or praying the sinner's prayer with a convert.

Witnessing is first and foremost something you *are*. Jesus' last recorded words on this earth prior to His ascension back to heaven are these: "You shall be witnesses to Me" (Acts 1:8).

Note the word "be." Jesus didn't say, "You shall do witnessing." He said you are to "be witnesses."

Your witness about Jesus is only as good as your relationship with Jesus and the extent to which you allow Him, through the power of the Holy Spirit, to indwell you.

## The Fact Is, You're Already a Witness If You Have Received Christ into Your Life

If you confess Jesus Christ today as your Savior and Lord, you are His witness. You don't have to become a witness about Him. You are already one.

The question is not, "Am I a witness?"

The question is, "What kind of witness am I?"

As a Christian, you do what you do because of who you are in Christ and who He is in you.

If you don't know who you have dwelling within you, then you will always try to become something or someone other than Jesus.

Let me put it this way . . .

- If you don't recognize that Jesus is righteousness dwelling within you, then you may spend years in frustration seeking to become more righteous. The fact is that you can't get any more righteousness than that which you already have in Jesus Christ who dwells within you by His Spirit.
- If you don't recognize that the author of all spiritual authority is dwelling within you, then you may find yourself attending a dozen seminars in a frantic search to have more spiritual authority. The fact is, you can't get any more spiritual authority than that of Jesus Christ whose Spirit resides within you.
- If you don't recognize that the source of all divine love is dwelling within you, then you are likely to become exhausted in your human efforts to be more loving. The fact is, all the love you could ever hope to have to share with others is already resident in Jesus Christ whom you have invited to indwell your spirit.

Many of us judge our salvation and righteousness by some kind of man-made, external standard of certain behaviors and qualifications. Forgiveness, however, isn't something you earn or display according to external man-made criteria. Forgiven is what you are when you have received the Lord

Jesus into your life. Righteousness, it follows, isn't something you earn. Righteous is what you are when you are forgiven by God.

Don't evaluate your ability or your qualifications to witness based on any type of skills you feel you have or don't have. View yourself as God sees you: a forgiven, righteous, fully alive representative of His Son. Jesus said, "Judge not according to the appearance, but judge righteous judgment" (John 7:24). In other words, you aren't to judge according to an outer, man-created standard, but you are to see things the way God sees things. God sees you as forgiven by His Son, and therefore, fully qualified to be a witness to His Son. He sees you as a capable witness to the gospel and the life-changing power of Jesus Christ.

Don't look at your deficiencies, separation, or weakness. Look at His strengths. He is the one who is flowing in and through you.

## Flowing Like a River

Jesus said, "He who believes in Me, as the Scripture has said, out of his heart [innermost being or "from within"] will flow rivers of living water" (John 7:38). Notice that Jesus said, "shall flow." You don't have to engineer the process. And yet, how many of us think that we are the ones who need to prime the inner pump or get things channeled. Rivers don't need to be made to flow; they need only be allowed to flow.

Stated another way, you don't need to "work up" witnessing in the same way that you might prepare a presentation, a project, or a performance. You simply need to allow Jesus within you to flow out to those around you as naturally as inhaling and exhaling.

A baby is born to breathe. It doesn't need to learn to breathe or take a course titled Oxygen Exchange 101. No, the baby opens its mouth for that first gasp of air at birth and breathes.

When you are born anew spiritually, you don't need to acquire the skill of witnessing. You simply need to let Jesus flow through you to others.

This is not to belittle or downplay the value of training skills. It is to say that skills *apart* from the anointing of the Holy Spirit have little value; skills acquired and submitted to the anointing of the Holy Spirit are, on the other hand, very valuable.

## Renewing His Flow

"But," you may say, "nothing seems to be flowing."

Then go back to Jesus. Don't turn to something man has created or engineered. Turn back to the Lord and trust His promise to you: "If anyone thirsts, let him come to Me and drink. He who believes in Me, as the Scripture has said, out of his heart will flow rivers of living water" (John 7:37–38). If nothing is flowing from you . . . drink more of Jesus. Renew your relationship with Him. Take a look again at the cross and what it means to your life and to your everlasting future. Take a look again at who is living inside you and in whom you are living.

When you renew your relationship with the Lord, you revitalize your capacity to give Jesus to the world around you. Nothing else can suffice in the same way as your going to the Lord and saying to Him, "I want to know You better and be filled with more of Your presence."

A noted spiritual leader Charles Trumball tells a story about seeing from a distance what appeared to be a man pumping water from a well in China. The water was flowing virtually nonstop as the man pumped vigorously. He said to himself, "I've got to meet a man who can pump water like that."

As he got closer he realized that the figure wasn't a man after all, only a wooden image of a man on a hinge connected to a water pipe. Furthermore, the water was flowing from an artesian spring and the arm-shaped hinge wasn't pumping the water, the water was flowing so that it pumped the figure's hinged arm!

That's what it means to me to have the life of Jesus flowing through me as a witness. I tried for five long and tiring years to "pump up" enough righteousness to share with others.

When I finally asked the Holy Spirit to flow within me, He started pumping me out to others.

## Flowing to Overflowing

I believe the early Church was so full of Christ and so full of the Spirit—they had believed and received so much—that their hearts were literally bubbling over with the Lord. They had such a flow of joy and peace and inner reality within them that they could not contain it. That which was inside them overflowed into their every conversation. Their conversations led to their actions. Their witness was a powerful one, as a result, and the Scriptures tell us, new souls were added daily. (See Acts 2:47.)

For many of us, the "confessing" of the Lord—the active ongoing witnessing about Him—is difficult because we simply aren't believing the right things about Jesus or because we aren't receiving enough of the Holy Spirit's provision into our lives so that we are filled to overflowing!

Jesus said,

He who believes in Me, as the Scripture has said, out of his heart [innermost being] will flow rivers of living water *(John 7:38)*.

Jesus also said,

Out of the abundance of the heart the mouth speaks *(Matthew 12:34)*.

Want flowing rivers of testimony? Believe for them! Receive the Holy Spirit who gives them!

Want a mouth that is speaking or confessing Christ in an abundant way? Have a heart that is bursting with belief and filled to overflowing with the Holy Spirit.

If Jesus Christ is truly real to you—if He is alive and bursting forth with His power, peace, love, and joy in your life— you will *want* to share Him with others. In fact, you'll find that you can't help but speak about Him and praise Him for the good things of your life. The Lord Himself taught, "Out of the abundance of the heart the mouth speaks. A good man out of the good treasure of the heart brings forth good things, and an evil man out of the evil treasure brings forth evil things" (Matthew 12:34–35).

## In Filling You with His Spirit, He Has Equipped You with Himself!

Let me share a few uplifting Scriptures with you:

Not that we are sufficient of ourselves to think of anything as being from ourselves, but our sufficiency is from God, who also made us sufficient as ministers of the new covenant, not of the letter but of the Spirit (2 Corinthians 3:5–6).

You don't need to know everything about the Bible in order to be a witness to Christ Jesus. You have already been made an able minister of the new covenant on account of what has happened in your spirit.

We are ambassadors for Christ (2 Corinthians 5:20).

You are an ambassador for the King of kings. That isn't just a positional or judicial truth. It's an actual truth—one that lives itself out in very practical ways as you begin to live out and apply what you know is true in His Word. You are an ambassador whether you believe it or not.

For if the firstfruit is holy, the lump is also holy; and if the root is holy, so are the branches (Romans 11:16).

You are holy because you are a branch joined with Jesus, the true vine. As Jesus said:

I am the true vine . . . . You are already clean because of the word which I have spoken to you. Abide in Me, and I in you. As the branch cannot bear fruit of itself, unless it abides in the vine, neither can you, unless you abide in Me. I am the vine, you are the branches. He who abides in Me, and I in him, bears much fruit; for without Me you can do nothing. . . . If you abide in Me, and My words abide in you, you will ask what you desire, and it shall be done for you. By this My Father is glorified, that you bear much fruit; so you will be My disciples (John 15:1, 3–5, 7).

No branch separated from its vine can survive for very long, much less produce new fruit. The same holds true for any plant separated from its roots. It will wither and die, and all of its fruit-producing potential will die with it. (We have a vivid example of that principle every Christmas season, don't we, when we see by early January how dead and brittle our cut "evergreen" branches and trees have become.)

When you abide in Jesus as a branch abides in a vine, you literally expect His life to flow into you and through you. You can accept that you are becoming more like Him every day—taking on His nature bit by bit, being ever transformed into His likeness. That's the only way you can fulfill what Jesus said in the Sermon on the Mount:

> Therefore you shall be perfect, just as your Father in heaven is perfect (*Matthew 5:48*).

"Perfect" in this passage means "whole" or "complete." The only way you can become complete is to allow Jesus to flow in you. You can't do it by yourself. You can't achieve wholeness. You can simply invite the only whole person who ever lived to indwell you by His Spirit and make you realize more of your wholeness day by day.

Will it happen? The New Testament declares:

> He who has begun a good work in you will complete it until the day of Jesus Christ (*Philippians 1:6*).

Jesus isn't going to give up on you. He will continue to work greater and greater wholeness in you until the day He returns to this earth to rule and reign. Count on it! Believe it! Trust God to do what He has said He will do!

You may not be all you should be today, but if you're walking in the Spirit, you're on your way to becoming even more like Christ.

You may not be the best witness for Christ Jesus today, but you are His witness and you're becoming an even more powerful and effective witness.

You may not know everything you'd like to know about Jesus or the gospel or how to win souls, but you're learning and growing. You're *becoming* who He has said you *are;* now believe and act in faith on what you believe.

# You Don't Earn Righteousness, You Are Righteousness

In Proverbs 11:30, we read these great words: "He who wins souls is wise."

Many of us have heard that phrase over the years of hearing about, and even participating in, various "evangelism drives." The first part of that verse often goes overlooked, however. The full verse reads:

> The fruit of the righteous is a tree of life,
> And he who wins souls is wise.

Who are "the righteous"? Jesus Christ has made righteous all those who have believed in Him and accepted His blood sacrifice as the only sacrifice necessary for the remission of their sins. If you have been born anew spiritually, you are "the righteous"!

Righteousness is not something you come up with, engineer, or produce in yourself. That's self-righteousness, and the Bible refers to it as being like "filthy rags." The true righteousness is that which comes from Jesus Christ. It works from the inside out. As Philemon 6 says, "I pray that you may be active in sharing your faith, so that you will have a full understanding of every good thing we have in Christ" (NIV).

We must each ask ourselves the question, "What is it in me that is good?"

The only truly good thing in us *is* Christ Jesus! Apart from Christ Jesus, there's nothing good in us, said the Apostle Paul: "For I know that in me (that is, in my flesh) nothing good dwells" (Romans 7:18).

However, if you are dwelling in the Spirit, Christ is in you and you are in Him. Therefore, all of His goodness is in you. It's up to you to acknowledge, or to confess, that goodness is part of who you now are as a follower of the Lord Jesus.

You may say, "But I don't feel very righteous." How you feel is beside the point. The Bible says that you are the righteous.

You may say, "But I don't always act very righteous. Sometimes I do things I know I shouldn't." Your mistakes, too, are beside the point. The reality of what you are on the inside will manifest itself in time as the Holy Spirit transforms you from within and old patterns of behavior begin to slough off you like dead skin cells do. You are being remade from the inside out.

Our culture is one that says, "I'll believe it when I see it." God's way of doing things, on the other hand, is such that believing results in seeing. Believe first, and then see the results of your belief. (See Hebrews 11:1.)

If you look for righteousness on the outside and expect your outward behavior to result in right standing with God, you'll search forever and never find.

However, if you believe that righteousness is who you are on the inside, righteousness based on faith will begin to manifest itself on the outside.

Righteousness simply doesn't seep from your actions into your spirit. It is a reality inside your spirit that is demonstrated in your behavior as you accept your own righteousness by faith. Righteousness moves from the inside out, not from the outside in.

Now how does all this relate to soul winning?

Very directly!

When you believe that you are a witness, then you act like a witness in new and creative ways.

If you don't believe that you are a witness, then you won't act like one.

What freedom you have! Your old self has been crucified and buried with Christ. You have been raised up with Him in newness of life and are walking a new path with Him. He calls you His righteousness. He promises to perfect you. You continue to walk in His path, however, not in your own strength, but in His.

## What You Have Within You!

The crucial issue is to live in Christ Jesus—in the glory and power of God—so that everything you say and do is a reflection of who He is. That, in turn, defines who you are. It puts

you in proper relationship to who He is. It fulfills why you are. And then, you need to know what you have.

It's not enough just to know the purpose of God for your life if you don't know the *provision* that God has made for us to fulfill that purpose. Assume for a moment that your purpose is to climb to the top of a very high mountain. Knowing your purpose isn't enough. You also need to know what provision will be made for you to have what you need to undertake the trek—provision for food, water, warmth, emergencies, proper gear and clothing, and so forth.

Salvation is not just forgiveness of sins and a secure pass to live in heaven someday. For many people, that's all salvation means. I felt that way for years. All I knew about salvation was that my sins were forgiven, and I'd go to heaven when I died.

Salvation involves so much more! Salvation doesn't only deal with the past and decide the long-range future. It provides for the here-and-now of our lives. Otherwise, we would each face a long dry spell in the desert of defeat from our salvation day to our death day—struggling in despair, with our only hope and consolation being that things weren't as bad as they once were and weren't as good as they were someday going to be.

If we view salvation that way, we'll miss the present tense of our salvation experience. All we'll have is a past experience and a hope for the future.

Let's consider for a moment just what our salvation means to us daily, this moment.

What we have now is Christ's life in us. If Jesus is *alive* in you, that means He's moving, doing, acting . . . *now!*

## He Never Said You Could Do It Alone

I was raised in Arkansas, and after I finished school, I went into the Air Force. I spent most of my four-year term of military service overseas. Actually, I traveled to some thirty countries during those years of service, and I returned to the states in 1968 feeling that I had seen everything the world had to offer. And yet, I had a restlessness in my life and in my heart;

I knew I was still searching for something I couldn't name.

I had grown up in a preacher's home, and I had heard the gospel and had accepted Jesus intellectually. In fact, I was baptized and joined the church when I was twelve years old. That wasn't enough, however. I didn't have a personal, spiritual connection with the Lord Jesus. Feeling this emptiness as a twenty-two-year-old who had traveled the world, I finally came to the place where I trusted the Lord completely and received Christ as my personal Savior and Lord.

For the next five years, I worked hard at doing all the things I was told a good Christian did. I was deeply committed to the Lord and my labor for Him was one of love. But it was also exhausting. And in my exhaustion, I was discouraged.

After five years, I had very few souls to show for all my attempts at witnessing. I was nearly burned out on Christianity. I had struggled and strived to live the "good life" and to do what I thought was required of me, and I was sick and tired of it all—especially tired. I had beaten myself against the wall of Christian good works until I was exhausted.

In desperation I cried out to the Lord, "If You've got something better, I'm ready to receive it."

He spoke deep within my heart, "Thanks. I've been waiting all this time for you to say that."

He showed me clearly that I didn't have to do the work. He'd do the work. He'd prepare the people. He'd show me where to go. He'd lead me in what to say. He'd do the convicting. And He'd do the saving. All I had to do was follow His lead.

When I began to trust Him to prepare the way, prepare my heart, orchestrate the encounters and the conversations, I began to see more people come to Christ *accidentally* than I'd ever been able to produce before *on purpose!*

## Born to Be a Soul Winner?

Some people say to me, "Well, certain people are just born with an inherent ability to win souls."

I don't believe that. The fact is that we each have been born again in our spirits to become a witness. In and of ourselves—in the flesh, as the Apostle Paul would say—none of us is a natural soul winner. In fact, we can't win souls apart from the Holy Spirit moving in us and through us to others.

No matter how polished, strong, or capable some seem, none of us can really do anything in our own strength. We all must admit someday that we have no power or authority to give ourselves another breath, another second, or another idea. We must confess, "I can't."

The good news is that when you admit you can't, God steps in and says, "I never said you could. But I always said I can and I will!"

You can't save yourself. He never said you could. He always said He would if you simply received Him.

You can't transform your own life into the image of Christ. He never said you could. But, He always said He would if you trusted Him to lead you, guide you, and change you.

You can't change another person's life. He never said you could. He always said He would if you planted a seed of the gospel.

## Seeking to Be a Soul Winner? Seek Christ

First seek Christ. Invite Him into your life. And then you no longer need to seek what He already is within you!

I hope you will let that truth sink deep into your spirit today. If you do, it will liberate you from a great deal of striving to become something that you already are: simply allow Jesus Christ to do His work in and through you.

I encourage you today: . . . *stop searching for a greater ability to witness and start releasing the nature of Christ that is already indwelling you!*

Being His witness means letting Him be, through you.

## Stop Striving and Start Releasing

The very premise for you to be a witness to Jesus Christ is for you to allow Him to do His work in you and to manifest His nature through you.

If you refuse to do that, you'll run in circles until you're ragged trying to get good enough to witness about the Lord. You'll always think there's more you should *have* or *know* before you begin to *give* the gospel to others. And the result will be that you never give.

Nearly every Christian I've ever met has a strong sense that he or she should witness. Some phrase it this way: "I know I should be doing more for the Lord" or, "I know I should witness more."

Once you come to a knowledge that your witness is what you are and that what you are is based entirely on who He is within you—and equally important, what you allow Him to be within you—then you can be free from that frustration!

You don't need to take a twenty-hour course in soul-winning before you say something to someone about Jesus Christ.

You don't need to memorize a hundred Scriptures or recite a sequence of spiritual laws or learn a new presentation technique before you bring up the name of Jesus in a conversation.

In fact, you don't even need to read the rest of this book before you witness about Jesus Christ (although I hope you will read this entire book for encouragement and instruction). You can put this book down right now and win thousands of people to the Lord simply by speaking what you know of Jesus who dwells within you by His Spirit and by allowing Him to work through your words about Him, your work for Him, and your worship of Him.

If you have invited Jesus to dwell within your spirit and have been renewed by the power of the Holy Spirit, then you already have everything you'll ever need to be a witness to Jesus Christ. When you've got Him, you've got all it takes to talk about Him and to act on His behalf!

Again, it's a matter of acknowledging that you have the living Christ dwelling within you and then putting yourself in a position to allow Him to operate through you to others.

## No Right Way—Only a Right Relationship

There's no right way to witness about the Lord. There's only a right relationship to have with Him—and once you have that right relationship, you have all the prerequisites you need for witnessing.

Read again what the apostle Paul wrote to the Corinthians: "For He made Him who knew no sin to be sin for us, that we might become the righteousness of God in Him" (2 Corinthians 5:21). In other words, Christ has become your righteousness and therefore, because He dwells in you, *you* are the righteousness of God. You don't have to go out and try to become something you already are.

In 1 Corinthians 6:17, the apostle Paul stated simply, "He who is joined to the Lord is one spirit with Him."

In other words, if you confess that Jesus Christ is your Savior and Lord, you have His spirit. You are joined with Him. You share one spirit. All that He is—His entire nature—is entirely available to you.

The good news is you don't have to get good in order to get God. Each one of us who has been reborn knows that. We know that while we were sinners, Christ died for us. He saved us from our sins when we acknowledged that we were sinners and repented of the willful acts that separated us from God. None of us became good enough to be rewarded with salvation. We were shown the mercy of God through our believing on Jesus Christ and accepting His shed blood as the sacrifice for our sins.

The same principle holds true for witnessing. You don't have to be good at being a Christian before you can be a witness. If you have Christ, you are one in spirit with Him and you have everything you need to be His witness. He operates in you and through you according to His mercy and His grace when you allow Him to operate by faith.

You accepted Jesus into your life by faith.

You release Him to the world, which is another way of saying that you are His witness, the same way—by faith.

## A Matter of Faith, Not Skill

All it takes to be a witness is to choose to live by faith and in faith. In other words, we must choose to put our trust in Him rather than in our own ability and to trust the consequences of our actions to Him.

This truth is tremendously freeing for many people I've met who would like to be witnesses but feel inadequate.

You took a risk of faith in accepting Jesus. You believed that when you confessed your sins, repented of them, and invited Jesus Christ to come into your life and fill you with His spirit, He would do it! You had faith that Jesus would be faithful to the promises in the Bible and that He would do what He said He would do on your behalf. Even today, you believe that you have eternal life. You believe your sins are forgiven. How do you believe it? By faith.

It takes a risk of faith to witness. You must believe that when you speak the truth of God, give a word about Jesus, or share a message about the gospel, then God will do what He said He would do—His Word will accomplish the purposes of God for which He sends it. We must:

- Believe that what God has said, He will do.
- Believe that what God has promised, He will fulfill.
- Believe that what God has declared to be true is true.
- Believe that what God says about you, you are.
- Believe that what God calls for you to do, He means for you to do.

When you begin to believe God and begin to trust Him to do what He has said in His Word, He converts a seemingly abstract truth into a truth that you experience and in which you live.

## Faith—All Along the Way

Just as it takes faith in Christ to become a Christian, it takes an ongoing faith in Christ to be a Christian. Just as Christ does the saving, so He does the maintaining and the growing within you.

You believe. He enters.

You receive. He manifests.

You confess who He is with your mouth. He transforms you into His likeness.

You'll find that principle again and again in the New Testament. The believing, receiving, and confessing are what you do. When you believe God—no matter what—He enters the situation to do His work. When you receive His Holy Spirit, He begins to work in a way that readily becomes visible and recognizable. When you confess who He is, He transforms you, and usually the situation or circumstances in which you find yourself, into what is pleasing to Him.

How does this relate to soul winning?

Before you'll ever choose to be an active soul winner you must believe that God wants to use you—to guide you, to work through you, to direct you, to speak through you—to save the lost. I believe that's what the Apostle Paul meant when he said, "As ye have therefore received Christ Jesus the Lord, so walk ye in him" (Colossians 2:6). You receive Him and He indwells you in order to work through you to bring others to Himself.

Furthermore, in order to be an active soul winner, you must receive the Holy Spirit and acknowledge the fact that He dwells within you. You must acknowledge His presence and invite Him to control your life and say to Him, "Lead me. Guide me. Use me. Direct me. Speak through me. Make yourself known to others through my life." Receiving is active, not passive. The Holy Spirit does not force Himself on you. You must trust the Holy Spirit to indwell you and use you.

And then, you must be willing to confess the Lord with your mouth. In other words, you must be willing to speak aloud about Him. You must give voice to what you believe. You must use His name and praise His name. You must *confess* Him.

## Confessing the Lord

What does it mean to confess the Lord? It means to tell the truth about what you know about Him. If you say, "I want to make a full confession," you are saying, "Here's the whole truth and nothing but the truth about what has happened. I want to tell it all."

To confess the Lord means that He becomes the number-one topic of your conversation. Everything you think, do, and talk about has its focal point in the Lord Jesus. He's the reason. He's the cause. He's the encourager. He's the empowerment along the way—for everything in your life! You can't help but talk about Him because He is your Lord, which means, literally, your master. You do His bidding. He is the one responsible for you. He is your rewarder and the one who gives you the provision, opportunity, and means to do

No matter what profession you're in, no matter what your schedule or agenda might be, no matter for whom you work or with whom you work or who works for you, no matter what product or service you provide or sell or deliver or market or produce, your Lord—the one who ultimately calls the shots in your life—is Jesus.

Believe.

Receive.

Confess.

The Lord compels you to activate this cycle of faith in your life almost continually, and as you obey and believe, receive, and confess, you grow in your faith.

As you grow, you produce spiritual fruit.

Producing fruit encourages you to believe for yet more, to receive even more, and to confess ever further. Faith becomes an ever-growing, ever-flowing, ever-rising cycle within us.

## "Confessing" Is Why God Needs You and Me

You may say, "Well, if this is God's work, why does He need me?"

It has always been God's desire to express Himself and to reveal Himself to and through His people. That's the story of the Bible. God desired to show His character through Israel, His chosen people. He still desires to express who He is, and He now does so through those who have received Him and acknowledge Him as their Lord.

It's God's divine and sovereign plan to reveal Himself in the lives of human beings and to have such intimate fellowship with men and women that they become more and more like Him as they allow Him to manifest Himself through their personalities, talents, traits, skills, and desires.

It's a great mystery *why* God would choose this method of proclaiming His presence in the world. The fact is that this *is* His method and we are invited to participate in it.

The greatest truth you can know about yourself is that you are destined to portray the truth about God to the world. You were designed to express His life. You cannot do what only God can do. That's a very important point. Jesus said, ". . . without Me you can do nothing" (John 15:5). On the other hand, God chooses to express Himself through people who are willing to allow God to use them.

## Why Am I?

Many people never know their purpose in life. If you are among them, I'd like to tell you what your purpose in life is.

In order to understand the purpose of your salvation, you must first begin to understand your purpose in creation. The Bible says:

> Then God said, "Let Us make man in Our image, according to Our likeness; let them have dominion over the fish of the sea, over the birds of the air, and over the cattle, over all the earth and over every creeping thing that creeps on the earth" *(Genesis 1:26)*.

We read in Isaiah 43:7: "I have created [believers] for My glory."

You were created in God's image and likeness. You were created to have dominion over this earth. You were created to bring glory to Him.

Sin separated you from that purpose. Your salvation through Jesus Christ has put you back in position to fulfill your purpose on the earth—to rule and reign through Christ Jesus.

You may note that God has never said in His word that you were created to win souls. Commanded by Jesus, yes. Created for that purpose, no.

The fact is, however, that if you are reflecting God's image and likeness to the world around you, you will be a soul winner. Those who are still in sin and are desiring to be free of the guilt of sin will be attracted to you as a moth is attracted to light.

If you are reflecting the glory of God, you will win souls. Your love for others, an extension of God's love for you, will be a magnet that hurting and suffering men and women will find irresistible.

If you are taking rightful spiritual dominion over this earth, exerting your God-given right over evil wherever you encounter it, you will win souls. Those who have been in the bondage of the enemy and whose eyes have been covered by scales of indifference will suddenly find themselves coming face to face with the reality of God's salvation.

Again, we come back to that idea of abiding in Jesus. Jesus is the only human being who completely manifested the glory of God and totally fulfilled His created purpose of being in the image and likeness of God with full dominion over the spiritual and physical realities of this world.

When Jesus lives in you, and you in Him, and when you are claiming all of what He purchased for you on the cross, then you are in a position to be what He created you to be: a fully alive, complete human being who is manifesting His image and likeness, bringing glory to God, and taking dominion over the enemy of our souls. That kind of person is a spontaneous soul-winner! Can you see how that is so? Such a person is irresistible! People you meet can hardly wait to find out how to be more like you. They can hardly wait to discover your secret to living. They are eager to know what you know and to have the inner life that you have.

## No Cookie-Cutter Job Description

Every person in today's business and professional world—indeed, in every segment of life—understands that there's more to an employee than a job description or an amount of productivity. Companies as well as governments, schools, churches, and communities, are made up of *people*. Each person brings to a job description certain qualifications, traits, and abilities. Those qualities determine to a great extent the person's motivation for doing a job, his steadfastness in pursuing it to its completion, and the amount of effort, energy, and enthusiasm he will give it.

Jesus Christ chose to indwell *your* humanity by His Spirit—to transform *you* so that through *your* life He might reveal His life to other people. In doing so, the Lord chooses to use your personality, your likes and dislikes, and your abilities, strengths, and desires as part of His method for reaching others.

Not every person who calls herself a Christian will manifest Christ in exactly the same way. There are no "cookie cutter" images of what a Christian will say or do in any one set of circumstances. God uses your creative ability to express yourself to bring others to Himself. He puts you in unique situations. He allows you to be totally and uniquely who you are as you convey Jesus Christ to the world.

Begin to see your soul winning as being unique to your personality. That's the way the Lord Jesus designed soul winning to work best.

Be who you are. Trust the Lord to personalize your soul-winning plan to reflect both who you are and who He is.

## Your Unique Plan

That means, of course, that *your* soul-winning approach will ultimately be uniquely your own. Nobody else can do your job just the way you can do it, because nobody else has the same qualifications, talents, skills, spiritual gifts, and past experiences that you do. And therefore, nobody else has your ideas and creative approaches. Furthermore, nobody else has the same set of motivations, the same desires, or the same personal goals and sense of purpose that you do.

What is true for your job, is also true for your work within your family and your church. It is equally true for your work in winning souls.

Don't expect to win souls in the same way that Susie or Sam does. Don't expect to win souls the same way that Jerry Wiles does. Do expect God to use you in a unique way to win the souls He puts across your path.

Soul winning involves a blending of who you are with who Christ is, to reach an individual who is at a particular point on her path toward Christ.

Even if you choose to use somebody else's ideas and plans as a springboard, you'll eventually find yourself wanting to make adjustments here and there to accommodate who you are. That's OK! Your best soul-winning plan is ultimately the one that God tailor makes for you.

You came to Christ in a unique way. Nobody else came to know Him in exactly the same way you did. By that I mean that nobody else had the same set of experiences and input that you had in coming to the point where you were ready to say yes to Christ, to seek forgiveness of your sins, and to be filled with Christ's own spirit.

Nobody else heard just those hymns, had just those conversations, went to just those services, heard just those sermons, or responded to just that altar call in just that way. That holds true even if you were one of thousands who went forward at a Billy Graham crusade. Each person who walks those aisles has a unique background that led him to get up out of his chair and make his way from the top row of the stadium to stand and pray a sinner's prayer on the twenty yard line.

Therefore, don't presume that every person you meet or with whom you share the gospel or the name of Jesus Christ will respond in exactly the same way.

Salvation is not a matter of "one formula fits all." It's a unique process for each person because each individual has a unique pattern of sin in his life, a sense of guilt that is related to a unique set of sinful behaviors, and a unique point at which that guilt becomes so burdensome that the message of salvation is not only accepted but eagerly desired.

## In the Flow of Your Life

It is in the flow of your unique life and personality that the Lord will bring people across your path so that you can confess Him in your unique way. Very specifically, anticipate these things.

- The people you encounter will be those within the normal everyday routine of your life. You won't have to go out of your way to meet them. They'll be in your path.
- The people you encounter will be those with whom you can readily establish a common interest or experience. This holds true even if you are talking with a janitor in your building or a maid working in a hotel where you are staying. They will be people with whom you can find a comfortable opening line of conversation.
- The people you encounter who are ready to meet the Lord Jesus and to accept Him as their Savior will be those with whom you easily establish rapport and understanding. Directing the conversation toward Christ will be natural for you. It will be thoroughly suited to the context of your life, their lives, and the work of Christ in the world.

Time and again we read in the New Testament that Jesus encountered people "as He went." Some of your most fruitful gospel-sharing encounters are going to come "as you go."

Live your life, allowing Him to live His through you.

Although the Lord may occasionally lead you to seek out someone, most of your opportunities to share Christ with others will be right before you as you walk out your life. You generally won't have to seek out opportunities. Your part, rather, is to . . .

- recognize the opportunities as they come, and
- to speak His name and ask the question, "Would you like

to receive Jesus Christ as your personal Savior and Lord?"

Everything else is the work of the Holy Spirit, whom the church has traditionally identified as "the Lord, the giver of life." He is the one who transforms a person from being lost to being saved.

As you see souls come to the Lord, beware of the tendency to say, "I won this person to Christ," or to say "I won three souls for the Lord." The better perspective is this: "I had an opportunity to share Christ with a person today, and the Lord gloriously saved him," or "The Lord brought three new souls into His kingdom today, and I had the privilege of witnessing to them and praying with them."

The joy of joys and the wonder of wonders is that the Lord invites us to be a part of the process. He wants us to have this degree of intimate, intense fellowship with Him. He is eager to share examples of His life-changing power with us. He longs for us to be a part of His kingdom-building activities. He invites us along for the greatest blessing we can ever know apart from our spiritual conversion.

Such an invitation! Such a privilege! How is it that so many of us fail to RSVP?

# THREE

# WHAT YOU HAVE TO GIVE

We are part of a culture that says, "Let's make things happen."

Our world runs according to power. Natural power. Human power. Emotional power. The power of ideas and systems.

When it comes to soul winning, however, there's nothing you can do to *make* a person receive Christ.

## You Can't Make a Person Receive Christ

You can lead people to the light. But only the Holy Spirit can compel them to open their eyes.

You can speak words of truth to others. But only the Holy Spirit can open their ears and their hearts to truly hear your message.

You can pray for people who don't know Christ. But only the Holy Spirit can quicken your prayers and bind them to those souls.

You can give people you meet opportunities to receive Jesus into their lives. But they must say, "Yes." And only the Lord can change their hearts.

You can lift up His name and share His gospel. But the transforming of souls is His work. He alone makes it happen.

When Jesus declared on the cross, "It is finished!" He was making the supreme statement of all time. He had done it all, paid it all, and borne it all. The result is that there's nothing we can do, in and of our own strength, to earn God's love, mercy, or forgiveness. The only thing we can do is to accept what Jesus has done and to acknowledge that the price He paid on the cross for our sins is sufficient for our redemption.

You are never in a position to say, "I did it"—about our salvation, about any miracle of God, or about the winning of a soul. The Lord alone does the transforming, life-changing work.

There are, however, three things that the Lord asks you to do, equips you to do, and waits for you to do:

- Pray,
- Give testimony of what receiving the Lord has meant in your life, and
- Share His Word.

The Lord will not do these things for you. They are your responsibility.

## Commanded to Pray

First and foremost, we are commanded to pray for harvesters. The Lord Jesus said to His disciples, "Pray the Lord of the harvest to send out laborers into His harvest" (Luke 10:2).

Pray today for active soul winners to have courage and boldness in their sharing with the lost. Pray that the Lord will call more and more people to become active soul winners. Pray for yourself that you might be used as a soul winner.

I firmly believe that the more you pray for the Lord to send harvesters into His field, the more you will be aware of the harvest, the more you will see the need for laborers, and the more you will be willing to become one!

## A Burden for Lost Loved Ones

Most Christians feel a burden—a sadness, a heaviness of heart, a deep concern—for their loved ones who haven't received the Lord into their lives. You may have shared the gospel with a loved one, but that person hasn't responded . . . yet. What are you to do?

Continue to pray.

Make certain, however, that you continue to pray as God would have you pray.

> Pray in faith. Expect the person to come to the Lord. Don't focus on the fact that your loved one is lost. Anticipate the day in which he will be saved. Look forward with faith to the joy and peace that will indwell your loved one when he does come to know Jesus as his personal Savior and Lord.
>
> Pray with praise. Thank God for what He is doing in the life of your loved one. He *is* at work! Don't pray with a defeated attitude. Pray with joy! Your loved one today is one day closer to salvation than she was yesterday.
>
> Pray asking the Holy Spirit for guidance. Simply pray, "Heavenly Father, show me how to pray. Reveal to me the specific things I need to pray for and about." Whatever comes to mind, pray about it. You may be surprised at some of the ways the Lord directs you to pray.
>
> Pray against the forces of darkness that are keeping your loved one blind to the truth and deaf to the gospel. Second Corinthians 10:4–5 tells us: "For the weapons of our warfare are not carnal but mighty through God for pulling down of strongholds, casting down arguments and every high thing that exalts itself against the knowledge of God, bringing every thought into captivity to the obedience of Christ."
>
> Pray against the enemy of your loved one's soul. Pray specifically that he will see the error of false doctrine, unbelief, atheistic teachings, and hatred, and that all false teachers in his life will be exposed for what they are.
>
> Pray with persistence. Pray and continue to pray. Jesus likened our persistence in prayer to a widow who went again and again to a judge, who eventually gave her justice because of her persistence rather than his agreement with her request!
>
> Pray for righteousness and all good things to come into your loved one's life. The Holy Spirit is the giver of life. Jesus said He came to give life "more abundantly" *(John 10:10)*.

I recently read an article in which a man suggested that we pray for our loved ones by saying, "I present [your loved one's name] to God in the name of the Lord Jesus." This, he suggested, was a means of declaring that the person was no longer in the enemy's camp, but was being held by the Lord and was in the process of being claimed by Him. What a wonderful image to hold in your mind as you pray—indeed, a wonderful reminder that God is more concerned about the salvation of your loved one than you are.

## Praying for the Lost You Have Not Yet Met

Although we all find it much more personal to pray for the lost souls of those friends and relatives we know and love, we can also ask God to give us compassion for lost people we don't know.

Pray first for a change in your own heart. Ask God to make you more aware of the suffering of humanity and to reveal to you the deep hurts of people you encounter.

As you watch people from afar in public places, pray for them. Ask God to work in their lives and to meet their needs.

All of this is in vain, of course, unless you truly believe that the Lord hears and answers prayer and that prayer is God's method for bringing about change on the earth. In praying for lost souls, you may need to come to grips with what you believe about prayer. Study prayer in the Scriptures. I believe you'll discover again and again these truths about prayer.

- Prayer strengthens you as a believer. As you pray and intercede for others, your own faith is built up and boldness wells up inside you.
- Prayer defeats the enemy in the spiritual realm that has held the person in bondage, thus preparing the way for the seed of the gospel you present to lodge deep within the person and take root. Second Corinthians 4:4 tells us that the "god of this age has blinded, [those] who do not believe, lest the light of the gospel of the glory of Christ, who is the image of God, should shine on them." You can pray specifically for a person that the "god of this world" will no longer have power to blind the person's mind.
- Prayer opens you up to the guidance of the Holy Spirit.

Before I ever open my mouth to speak to another person about the Lord, I pray for that person. Quickly, silently, but nonetheless intensely. I pray that the Lord will guide me as I speak and that He will give me His words to say. I pray that I might be sensitive to His leading. I pray that good fruit will result from the conversation. All of that can be asked very simply and directly by praying, "Lord, help me." The Lord knows the intent of your heart and your deepest desires.

Prayer invites the Holy Spirit to work in a situation—both in your life and in the life of the person to whom you are about to speak.

## Praying with a Fellow Believer

From time to time, you'll find that the person with whom you bring up the name of Jesus is, indeed, already a believer in Him. Encourage that person in the Lord. Use your time with them to build up their faith.

You will probably find that most of the Christians with whom you enter into conversations are hurting in some way. Some have fallen away from a vital, strong relationship with the Lord. They frequently are eager to return to the Lord and to renew their commitment to Him, although they may have been embarrassed to go forward during a church service, reluctant to talk to their pastor, or afraid for some reason that God would no longer hear their personal petition. In many cases, they are relieved that someone has opened up the issue with them and is willing to pray with them that they might enter again into the sweet fellowship of feeling God's forgiveness and experiencing His presence. What a joy it is to help the backslider "slide back" toward the Lord!

Others are experiencing a problem—a struggle against the enemy—and your expression of faith and agreement in prayer bolsters their resolve to stand firm for the Lord Jesus and to take authority over the evil that is coming against them.

Others are simply tired. The devil's constant barrage of lies has worn them down. The illness of others, or in their own lives—whether physical, emotional, or mental—has wearied them. Your prayer with them will buoy them up and give them the strength and courage to continue to fight the fight of faith.

## Prayer Is Always Appropriate

Prayer is always an appropriate response—for both lost and "found" souls. Make prayer your first priority in soul winning. As you pray, your will develop a compassion for the lost. Your desire to see them receive the Lord will grow. Your priorities will shift toward a greater concern for soul winning.

In addition to praying, the Lord compels you to share with others your personal stories about what the Lord has done and is doing in and through your life.

## What Is Your Testimony?

Can you state in clear, straightforward terms today what Jesus Christ has done for you personally?

To confess the Lord Jesus means to "speak out" what you believe in your heart about Him and to tell what you know to be true about Him—*in your own experience.*

You may have a feeling in your heart about what the Lord has done for you but have never put that feeling into words. I encourage you today: practice giving your testimony!

Begin by giving your testimony to yourself. Get by yourself somewhere and have a conversation with yourself. Put into words what Jesus has done for you and what He means to you. Speak your testimony aloud! Talk it out.

## An Ordinary Conversion Story Will Do Just Fine!

We are apt to think of people who have highly dramatic or spellbinding before-and-after testimonies as being "special" in some way as soul winners.

Your ability to win souls isn't related to the drama of your testimony. You don't need to have been saved from a rough, hard-core, on-the-brink-of-disaster life in order to influence people to come to the Lord. In truth, we all were on the brink of disaster and eternal damnation as sinners before coming to the Lord, no matter what our outward behavior or circumstances were. The strength of your testimony lies in what Jesus went through for you, not on what you went through before you met Him and invited Him to be your Savior and Lord!

## You Can't Talk About a Relationship You Don't Have

Many people I meet have an acceptance of the historical Christ, but they do not have a personal relationship with Him and have not been born by the Spirit of God.

I frequently find after I've led someone to the Lord and prayed with him that he has been a member of a church for years, and yet, this is the first time he's ever felt as if he has had a personal conversation with the living Lord or invited Him to indwell his life with His saving, life-giving power.

I understand that.

I was a member of a church for years. My father is a pastor and I was inoculated at an early age with all of the right procedures and terminology about Jesus. Still, during all of those years in which I would have said yes to the question, "Are you a Christian?" I did not have a personal relationship with Jesus as my Savior and Lord.

It's extremely difficult to introduce someone to a person you don't know! It's a little like my knowing the president of the United States.

True I know the name of the president of the United States. I know many people who know him personally. I've been in the office where he works. I know how he was elected and many of the duties with which he occupies his time. I can describe his relationship with the Senate and the House of Representatives and his Cabinet and the Supreme Court. But, if you ask me, "Do you personally know the president of the United States?" I'd have to tell you, "No, not personally."

Furthermore, if you asked me to introduce you to the president, I'd have to say, "I can put you in touch with someone who might be able to do that for you, but I can't personally introduce you to him."

The relationship I don't have with the president of the United States is very similar to the relationship I didn't have with the Lord Jesus Christ for many years. I went to church. I could recite verses from the Bible. I knew the church's position on many issues. I knew people who did know Jesus Christ personally. But, I didn't know Him, and therefore, I had no basis on which to introduce Him to someone else. I might invite a person to church just as I might persuade someone to vote for a presidential candidate. But I couldn't get others into Heaven's throne room any more than I could have gained their entrance into the Oval Office.

If that's your situation, today, let me invite you to meet Jesus personally and to invite Him into your life to become your Friend of friends and Lord of lords.

You can do that by praying this prayer aloud:

*Heavenly Father, I accept right now what Jesus did on the cross for me. I accept His shed blood as the sacrifice for my sins. I admit to You that I am a sinner, and I ask You to forgive me of my sins and to cleanse my inner soul of the guilt I feel for them. Fill me with Your Spirit, today, I ask, and help me to live a new life as You lead me and guide me. Give me the inner power and strength that I need to live in a way that is pleasing to You. I turn my life over to You completely right now, and I trust You to do with me whatever is good and pleasing in Your sight. I pray this in the Name of Jesus. Amen.*

# A Testimony Is More than Theology

Your personal testimony should be one you can state in very clear and simple terms. It should be the story that could be headlined: "What Happened to Me One Day." It's the story of how you came to know Jesus, and it should always be told in the first person. Nobody else's personal testimony will be just like yours. Here's a brief example:

I was once miserable because I knew that I was a sinner. I felt a tremendous amount of guilt in my life. I knew I wasn't in a good relationship with God.

Then one day someone talked to me about Jesus and I found myself saying, "I want the kind of relationship with Jesus that this person has." I asked him what I should do and when he told me, I did it.

Here's what I did:

I prayed a simple prayer. I asked God to forgive me of my sins and to cleanse my soul. I trusted Jesus Christ as my personal Lord and Savior, and I asked Him to fill me with His Holy Spirit so that I might be a changed person on the inside. I didn't see flashing lights or hear any clanging bells, but I did believe what I was praying with all my heart and a deep feeling of peace came inside me at that time. That feeling has never left me. I asked the Lord to help me to understand His Word and to show me how to live for Him. I'm learning more about that every day.

I've got a real sense of joy in my heart now that I didn't have before. I've got a feeling of confidence in the future. I'm looking forward to living forever with the Lord in Heaven. I wouldn't trade what happened that day for anything in the world.

In summary, be able to tell in everyday language your own story of what led you to receive Jesus as your personal Savior and what difference that experience has made in your life. Be able to tell people what you believe about Jesus and why.

# Explore What You Believe About Jesus

Interview yourself. Explore how it is that you know what you know about Jesus. Ask yourself why you believe what you believe. The very evidence you give to yourself is the evidence that you have within you to share with someone else! Here's a brief example of the type of process I'm encouraging you to pursue:

*Jesus Christ has saved me from my sins.*
*How did He do that?*
*By dying on the cross. He took my place on the cross.*
*Why did I deserve a place on a cross?*
*Because I was a sinner. God cannot look upon those who have a sin nature. He is a good, just, and righteous God and He cannot accept sin. In order to be acceptable before God, I have to stand before Him sin-free. The penalty for those who choose to live as sinners is death.*
*Why did Jesus take my place?*
*Because He is the only one who has been qualified to do so. He was God's own Son and the Bible tells us that He was sin-free. He was God's chosen method as a sacrifice for my sin.*

*Why did it have to be a cross and be death?*
*Because from the foundation of the world, God established the princi-*
*ple that life is in the blood.*

And so forth!

As you converse with yourself about your own salvation and your own relationship with the Lord Jesus, you may want to have a Bible handy so you can look up verses that relate to what you are saying. Use a concordance to help you find verses that back up your beliefs.

Carry on a dialogue with yourself. Verbalize aloud. You'll find that the more you converse with yourself about who Jesus is—and very specifically, who He is to you and why you believe what you believe—two things will happen.

- First, what you believe about Jesus will be reinforced in your heart.
- Second, you'll become fluid in speech about the Lord. You'll become familiar with phrases and lines of thought so that they become a part of your thinking process, and as such, a normal part of your conversation.

This happens in a special way as your beliefs are reinforced by Scripture and as you rehearse Scripture to yourself. The Word will build you up. You'll discover that you are memorizing it even as you are rehearsing it. You'll find later that the Holy Spirit will bring verses to your mind as you are bold to . . .

## Share the Word of God

The Bible is God's Word. It is your foremost reference tool in sharing the gospel with others.

From cover to cover, the Bible points to Jesus. The Old Testament gives supporting evidence and background about who the Messiah is, shows the need for Him, and prophesies His coming and His work.

The New Testament confirms the Old Testament. It tells who Jesus was and is, what He said, how He works, and what we as Christians can do to reflect Him to others.

The Word of God is just that . . . the word that the Lord has spoken to *us*. It's for today. It's for you and me. It's for today's circumstances, problems, and needs.

The gospel—which literally means "good news"—is just that! It is the good news that Jesus came and died for our sins so that we could be forgiven and restored to a full and right relationship with our heavenly Father. It is the good news that Jesus rose from the dead so that we might live forever. It is the good news that Jesus has sent His Holy Spirit to indwell us and live His life through us. Whenever we share about the Lord Jesus or share a verse of Scripture with someone, we are sharing God's Word and good news.

There's power in sharing the Word of God that few of us acknowledge and none of us fully understands. The apostle Paul wrote, "For I am not ashamed of the gospel of Christ, for it is the power of God to salvation to everyone who believes, for the Jew first and also for the Greek." The Word of God is what brings people to salvation and to the point of believing.

When you share with others about Christ, you can always preface your remarks with what you know to be true from God's Word.

> *God's Word says that Jesus is the Way, the Truth, and the Life.*
>
> *God's Word says that Jesus died for your sins, so that you wouldn't have to bear the punishment for them.*
>
> *God's Word says that Jesus was resurrected from the dead as the first-born of all who would be resurrected. Therefore, God's Word is saying that you and I can be resurrected, too. We can have eternal life. Jesus bought that for us on the cross.*
>
> *God's Word says that when we believe in Him, we receive eternal life.*
>
> *God's Word says that when we repent of our sins and immerse our lives in the Lord, He fills us with His Spirit—and with that, His joy and peace.*
>
> *God's Word says that when you confess Jesus Christ as Lord, you are saved from eternal death and given eternal life.*

Yes, the most effective tool you have in your soul-winning arsenal is the Word of God!

## Hide the Word in Your Heart

In order to be able to share the Word of God with others, you must first, of course, have it in your heart to give. You must either memorize those verses that are key to your expression of who Jesus is or be able to turn to them quickly in a New Testament that you carry with you.

When Jesus encountered the men on the road to Emmaus, the Scriptures say that "beginning at Moses and all the Prophets, He expounded to them in all the Scriptures the things concerning Himself" (Luke 24:27).

As you read your Bible, note those verses that you might use in sharing with someone an answer to the question, "Who is Christ Jesus?"

Underline those passages. Read them again and again. Ponder them in your heart. Meditate upon them. Discuss them with other Christians. Come to a sure resolution in your own heart about who Jesus is and who you are in Him.

If you are questioning who Jesus is, I recommend to you that you read these four books of the Bible:

- The Gospel of John
- The First Epistle of John
- The Epistle of Paul the Apostle to the Romans
- The Epistle of Paul the Apostle to the Colossians

These four books focus on who Jesus is. Read and reread them until you feel you really *know* Him.

## Expect to Use the Word—and Expect It to Work

Hebrews 4:12 tells us, "For the word of God is living and powerful, and sharper than any two-edged sword, piercing even to the division of soul and spirit, and of joints and marrow, and is a discerner of the thoughts and intents of the heart." It is the Word of God that cuts through every argument and every excuse and brings a person to face himself squarely, and in so doing, to see his need for the Lord.

Frequently as I share with people what the Lord has done in my own life, I read or quote such verses as these:

- "Jesus said to him, 'I am the way, the truth, and the life. No one comes to the Father except through me'" (John 14:6).
- "Nor is there salvation in any other, for there is no other name under heaven given among men by which we must be saved" (Acts 4:12).
- "If you confess with your mouth the Lord Jesus and believe in your heart that God has raised Him from the dead, you will be saved. For with the heart one believes unto righteousness, and with the mouth confession is made unto salvation" (Romans 10:9–10).

Don't zip through the recitation of a verse by rote. Share it slowly and meaningfully. I find it very beneficial to personalize it. "Jesus says to you, too, Sam, 'I am the way for Sam; I am the truth for Sam; I am the life for Sam. Sam cannot come to the Father except by Me.'" Or, "Nor is there salvation in any other, Janet, for there is no other name under heaven given among men by which Janet must be saved."

God's word is universal; it is also extremely personal.

## Stay with Foundational Truths

What are the foundational truths you need to share with a person in order to bring him to Christ?

The real issues are:

- How much does a person need to know in order to receive Christ as his or her personal Savior and Lord?
- How much do *you* need to know in order to become fruitful and effective in your ministry, including leading others to Christ?

Many of us have held the idea that coming to Christ is a complicated matter—that a person must know a great deal in order to make a decision for Christ that will be lasting and sure.

Even if we believe that coming to Christ is a relatively simple manner, others of us have held to the idea that we must be highly trained, skilled, and experienced before we can lead others to Christ. That belief tends to put soul winning out of the realm of a spiritual pursuit into the realm of an intellectual activity.

The fact is that a person needs to know very little in order to receive Christ.

Similarly, a person needs to have very few skills in order to lead others to Christ. A person does not need seminary training, a year of Bible school, or a three-month training course. In many cases, I've led a person to Christ and have then helped that person immediately turn to a peer and lead her to Christ.

## What Is It That a Person Needs to Know?

A person needs to know five basic things:

- Sin kills
- Christ died for our sins
- Christ rose from the dead so we might live
- Every person needs to be born anew in spirit
- Every person can be born anew by asking Jesus to come into his life

All of these things come together when you concentrate your sharing of God's Word on the cross. The cross is at the center of your message to others. It must always be so. Then, and only then, do you have a firm basis for sharing the Lord with others.

## The Whole Cross and Nothing but the Cross

What is it that you are to say to others?

Thousands upon thousands of phrases are possible. In all of the conversations I've had with people about the Lord down through the years, I've never had a duplicate conversation. We are unique people. Our situations are always unique in time and space. The context for each conversation is unique. Our ability to use language is a creative gift from God. We rarely express ourselves in exactly the same way.

At the same time, all of our messages about the Lord Jesus have their focus in the cross.

The apostle Paul—the greatest soul winner described in the New Testament—said this about his message to spiritually lost men and women: "We preach Christ crucified" (1 Corinthians 1:23). He also said, "God forbid that I should boast except in the cross of our Lord Jesus Christ, by whom the world has been crucified to me, and I to the world" (Galatians 6:14).

To Paul, the cross was everything. It was the motive for his sharing Jesus with others. It was the central point of his message. It was the origin of his life.

The same is true for you.

The Christ of the cross is your message. It's really the only message that counts.

- It's what Jesus did on the cross that makes the difference between eternal life and eternal damnation, between heaven and hell.
- It's our place on the cross with Him that frees us from our old life of sin to enter into a newness of life.
- It's the cross that makes possible a genuinely loving, fully restored relationship with God, and also a loving, fully reciprocal relationship with another person.
- It's the shed blood of Jesus on the cross that saves us from who we are and transforms us into all that we can be.
- It's the cross that makes possible the church.
- It's our acceptance of what Jesus accomplished on the cross that puts us into a position to experience the manifold grace of God and an *abundance* of life (as promised in John 10:10).

Yes, the cross is the crux of every issue that is important to the existence of human beings!

Everything else of a religious nature that we might say to another person is peripheral to the cross.

Equally true, everything else of a spiritual nature that we strive to do or be, apart from the cross, will fall short.

## The Holy Spirit Bears Witness to the Word

As you share the truth of the Lord, the Word of God, and above all, the message of the Cross with a person, the Holy Spirit will bear witness to the truth in the person's heart.

As I share verses of Scripture with a person, I frequently ask, "You know that to be true, don't you?" It's only on rare occasion that a person will say no. The Holy Spirit works in the other person's heart so that she knows there's a ring of truth and of authority in what you are saying to her. She may put up a wall around her heart, but she knows, nevertheless, that she has heard a true word.

Which brings us back to our central theme.

The Holy Spirit can only quicken to another person what we are willing to share. It's not enough to pray. It's not enough to know the Scriptures. It's not enough to have a personal testimony. It's not enough even to know what you believe about the Lord *unless* you are willing to open your mouth and share it.

Confessing Christ—actually speaking out His name and sharing news about Him—has no substitute.

Consider for a moment the clouds of the sky. In Texas, where I now live, the people have a name for large, cumulus thunderheads that pass by without leaving a drop of rain. They call them "empties."

We as Christians can be like those clouds. We can look like rain bearers. We can be moisture-laden. But unless we empty our rain on the earth, we have no impact on the parched dry souls of our fellow human beings.

In my opinion, one of the best passages for any Christian to study—and even to memorize—is Isaiah 55:10–11, which declares:

> For as the rain comes down, and the snow from heaven,
> And do not return there,
> But water the earth,
> And make it bring forth and bud,

> That it may give seed to the sower
> And bread to the eater,
> So shall My word be that goes forth from My mouth;
> It shall not return to Me void,
> But it shall accomplish what I please,
> And it shall prosper in the thing for which I sent it.

What an encouragement that verse should be to all of us! When we speak God's Word—either something from the Bible or a Spirit-inspired *rhema* word of God to others—that Word is life-bearing. It *will* hit God's target. It *will* be used by God in His efforts to expand His own kingdom. It *will* be worthy.

Thus, we can have the full assurance that WHATEVER we say that lifts up the name of Jesus will be as good seed on this earth.

We do the watering. He does the growing. This principle is stated yet another way in the Bible.

## We Do the Lifting, He Does the Drawing

Jesus said, "And I, if I am lifted up from the earth, will draw all peoples to myself" (John 12:32).

Our job is to lift up Jesus.

His job is to draw men unto Himself.

When you speak the name of Jesus to a person in need, you are lifting up Jesus.

When you introduce Jesus into a conversation, you are lifting up Jesus.

When you reply with the words of Jesus (which you have learned from the Bible or which He gives you to speak at that moment), you are lifting up Jesus.

Most of us will talk to people readily about: the weather, the latest song we've heard or movie we've seen, sports news, our jobs, our hobbies.

We'll talk about the latest political or economic news, our most recent purchase, our families, our careers, work, and colleagues.

Yet none of those things is eternal. None of those topics gives a person an opportunity to know Jesus and to experience the life He has to give. None of these things can result in everlasting life for the hearer.

It's only when we lift up Jesus that He can draw men to Himself. And the truth is, when we do, He does!

The words we speak about Jesus are like welcome drops of water on the parched souls of humanity. They cause eternal seeds within to sprout and bring forth life.

Rather than talk about the weather, let's rain on somebody's soul today by sharing God's Word.

We lift Him up. He draws.

## It Only Takes a Spark

It only takes a spark to start a forest fire.

The words you speak to a person may not seem to be all that spectacular to your own ears. They may be words that you are sure the other person has heard many times. You may not even feel a particular unction as you speak. And yet, the miracle of hearing may very well occur for that person. That's the result of the Holy Spirit's preparing his ears to hear.

Consider the example of lighting a match in order to light a candle. If the wick on the candle isn't ready to receive a flame, the match will blaze and die. The failure to light the candle does not lie in the match, but in the candle. And even if the match fails to light the candle, it has—for one brief moment—provided light. So it is with your words. Even if the other person doesn't receive your words, the words have been spoken as rays of light into darkness.

Who knows who may have overheard your words? Your prayer? The verse you gave? The word of testimony you shared?

And even more importantly, who knows the ability of the spirit to hear what the mind refuses to hear?

# FOUR

# MAKING THE CHOICE TO BE AN ACTIVE SOUL WINNER

According to surveys, more than ninety percent of all Christians never lead even one person to Jesus Christ.

I find that sad, especially when so many people are hungering and thirsting for the words of eternal life.

## Why Aren't You Putting God to the Test?

A man recently said to me, "I pray all the time for souls and that God will use me to bring people to Christ, but I don't know if I'd ever have the nerve to ask a question like that."

I said to Him, "I think it's about time you put the Lord to the test."

He said, "What do you mean?"

I said, "Well, if you've been praying that He'd use you to win souls, how are you going to know if He's answering your prayer unless you open up a conversation with others about the Lord?"

He didn't say anything, but I could see the gears spinning in his mind, so I continued, "The Lord may have put dozens of people across your path, carefully arranging and orchestrating their lives just so they'd be in close proximity with you—people whose hearts were ready to accept Christ Jesus and be born anew spiritually. How will you ever know what the Lord is doing if you don't test the situation by speaking up and asking people if they have been thinking about the Lord lately?"

He said, "I never thought of it that way."

Most people don't. They are more afraid of sharks swimming in the waters of unentered conversations than they are joyful at the prospect that drowning souls might be saved from those waters!

Stop to think about it for a minute. The Lord is far more concerned about bringing people to His Son than you are. He wants people to be saved from eternal damnation and put on the path toward eternal life far more than you do.

If, indeed, you have been praying in faith that God would use you to win souls, why wouldn't the Lord cause people to gravitate your way

- to take a different route home so their path will intersect with yours?
- to stop to pick up a loaf of bread in the same store that you've stopped at for a bottle of milk?
- to be called in an emergency to do a double shift just so they'll be available when you arrive on the scene?
- to be the clerk who responds to you in a store filled with clerks?
- to come to the airport and get you as a passenger, rather than any of a thousand other travelers?

If you have made yourself available to the Lord to be a soul winner, He is no doubt delighted that you're available so He can send people your way for just that purpose! Trust Him to arrange the circumstances and the encounters. Ask Him to do so. Then act on the opportunities. You can't know if the Lord has sent a person your way unless you put the situation to the test by opening up a conversation about Christ Jesus.

## Active Soul Winning

Active soul winning is intentional.

As we've stated repeatedly in the first pages of this book, a witness is what you are. Your witness flows from your being in Christ. You are a witness to Him through your every action and word.

Active soul winning, by comparison, involves a focus and a commitment of your will.

Let's assume for a moment that your grandfather taught you at an early age how to fish and that you have spent many Saturday mornings with your grandfather fishing at a nearby lake. If a person came up to you and said, "Are you a fisherman?" your response would no doubt be yes. Not only do you know how to fish, but you have fishing gear and you have been fishing and you enjoy fishing. Therefore, you consider yourself a fisherman or fisherwoman.

What happens, however, if someone asks you, "Have you been fishing lately?" Your answer will be yes or no depending on how recently you've been to the lake (and how you define the word *lately*).

The same holds true for our Christian witness. If someone asks you, "Are you a Christian witness?" the answer is most assuredly, "Yes!" You are a Christian witness twenty-four hours a day, every day, no matter where you are or in what circumstance you may find yourself. A good witness or a bad one. Nevertheless a Christian witness.

However, if someone asks you, "Have you gone soul winning lately?" your answer will be yes or no based on how recently you engaged in active soul winning.

## Active Soul Winning Is Intentional

Active soul winning is not accidental. (Some witnessing opportunities, however, are accidental, at least from our human viewpoint. There are those times when we find ourselves sharing about Christ almost before we have time to think about what we are saying.)

Active soul winning involves

- a frame of mind—that you are going to share Christ at every opportunity
- a perspective on the world—that most people in the world need to hear the good news of Jesus Christ

- an intent of the heart—that you will share Jesus with every person with whom you can and with as many people as possible
- a focused concentration—that you continually will be on the alert for someone with whom you might converse about the Lord Jesus
- a purpose—that all of your words and deeds will be aimed at leading a person to a personal relationship with the Savior

Let's return to our fishing analogy for a moment. After all, Jesus did call His disciples to become "fishers of men" (Mark 1:17).

Catching fish doesn't happen by accident. Fish don't just leap out of a pond or lake and land on your doorstep fifteen miles away.

To catch fish you must

- First, decide that you are going fishing. A fisherman sets his mind and heart toward that activity. He says, "I'm going fishing."
- Second, get to a body of water where you believe you'll find fish. The fisherman puts himself into position to catch fish.
- Third, choose a spot. It might mean choosing a depth if you are trolling the lake, but even so, you will gravitate toward certain coves and inlets. Nearly every fisherman has a favorite "fishing hole" that is in one location of a lake, pond, stream, or river.
- Fourth, prepare your gear and your bait for the type of fish you are attempting to hook. And cast in your line!

Each of these principles is directly related to soul winning.

## Decide That You're "Going Soul Winning"

Adopt a mind-set that says, "I'm going to be continually on the alert for someone with whom I might share the gospel."

So few people have adopted this mind-set. And yet, it's the number-one step to active soul winning.

I'm talking about something far more than saying, "Let's go door-to-door with tracts on Tuesday night next week." Granted, that's an intentional approach. It's also much more limited than what I am suggesting.

I'm suggesting that you have a "going soul winning" perspective every hour of every day.

- When you take that out-of-town business trip, expect to come home and tell your family about the "fish" you caught for the Lord Jesus.
- When you go into a store, expect to share Christ with someone.
- When you eat out at a cafe, expect to open up a conversation with the waitress or waiter about the Lord.

This isn't an automatic response to your life in Christ. To adopt a soul winning mind-set is to *train your mind* to think this way. It's not a habit that comes with your spiritual conversion. It's a habit that comes through both the transforming of your life by the power of the Holy Spirit *and* your disciplining of your own mind.

Active soul winning is a choice of your will. It's *intending* to win souls. It's setting your face and your life toward that activity. It's *deciding* to become a soul winner.

Once you decide to be an active soul winner . . .

## Expect Your Steps to Be Directed

The Word of God also says, "A man's heart plans his way; / But the LORD directs his steps" (Proverbs 16:9).

When you make a commitment to be an active soul winner, that's an act of "devising your way." You are setting your heart, your will, toward soul winning. And when you do, the Lord will direct your specific steps, setting up individual encounters for you and putting people into your path whose hearts are prepared to accept the message you have to give.

The hurdles you encounter on that path are generally going to be ones that you put there.

## What Excuse Are You Using?

During the 1984 Olympics, I encountered a young man who was a victim of cerebral palsy. His name was Barney, and I'll never forget him. He had a pronounced limp and slurred speech. Slowly and with great labor, he told me that he had asked the Lord to take him home. He no longer wanted to live in his imperfect body. The Lord spoke deep in my spirit, "Tell him that I will grant his request. From now on, it won't be him living in his body, but Me living there and working through him. Tell him to speak My words and to tell others about My life, not his."

Barney obeyed the Lord's words to him. Though his speech was still labored, he began to share what the Lord meant to him with any one who would listen. Several people found Jesus through the love that flowed through Barney during those two weeks of Olympic games. Beyond that, Barney was a tremendous example to my entire witnessing team.

What obstacle do you feel you have to overcome before you can be an effective witness? It surely can't be any greater than the one Barney faced. Let the Lord conquer that barrier in you.

I'd like to cover several of the foremost hurdles that I see people putting in their paths. The first is . . .

## The Hurdle of Time

People sometimes say to me, "I'd like to win souls, but my schedule is full. I just don't know where I'd find the time."

I met a man in a restaurant one day as we were both sitting at the counter. After we had talked about several other things, I asked him, "Have you noticed any signs of spiritual awakening in this area?"

He said, "What do you mean?"

I said, "Have you noticed that people are becoming more aware of their need for the Lord these days?"

He said, "Yes, I have."

I then said, "Have you become aware of your own need for the Lord Jesus Christ?"

He said, "Yes, I know I need the Lord."

"Well," I said, "today is the day for you to invite Him into your life. We can pray together right now, if that's all right with you." We prayed together there at the counter in a prayer that he repeated after me:

"Heavenly Father,"
*"Heavenly Father,"*

"Have mercy on me a sinner."
*"Have mercy on me a sinner."*

"I accept what your Son, Jesus Christ, did on the cross when He died for my sins so that I don't have to be punished for them."
*"I accept what your Son, Jesus Christ, did on the cross when He died for my sins so that I don't have to be punished for them."*

"I ask You to forgive me of my sins."
*"I ask You to forgive me of my sins."*

"Fill me with Your Spirit."
*"Fill me with Your Spirit."*

"And help me to live a new life that is pleasing to You."
*"And help me to live a new life that is pleasing to You."*

"Give me Your peace and joy"
*"Give me Your peace and joy"*

"and the assurance that I have eternal life."
*"and the assurance that I have eternal life."*

"Help me to read my Bible and to talk to You on a daily basis."
*"Help me to read my Bible and to talk to You on a daily basis."*

"Thank you for accepting me right now as Your child."
*"Thank You for accepting me right now as Your child."*

"I pray in Jesus' name. Amen."
*"I pray in Jesus' name. Amen."*

How long does it take?

Our conversation about Christ and our prayer together took no more than two and a half minutes. (Read it aloud—both parts—and time it for yourself!)

It doesn't take long for a person to receive the Lord and for the Holy Spirit to "birth" a child into the kingdom.

Surely you can find two or three minutes a day for the most important work you can ever do on this earth?

Beyond the hurdle of "lack of time" is an even more common one . . .

## The Hurdle of Timidity

Many people become suddenly shy when it comes to talking about the Lord Jesus. These same people may be very free in expressing personal problems to others, or in asking questions, or in expounding on a favorite topic—even to total strangers. Bring up the possibility of mentioning the Lord to a friend or stranger, however, and their knees go weak.

If you are feeling too shy, weak, or "backward" to share the Lord with others . . .

## Pray for Boldness

The apostle Paul, whom many regard as the boldest of all preachers in the first century, prayed for boldness and asked others to pray that he might speak boldly about Christ.

In his letter to the Ephesians, Paul vividly describes the "whole armor of God" and our need to wear this armor as we fight against "spiritual hosts of wickedness in the heavenly places" and "withstand in the evil day." What are we to do once we have donned this armor? "Praying always with all prayer and supplication in the Spirit, being watchful to this end with all perseverance and supplication for all saints—and for me, that utterance may be given to me, that I may open my mouth boldly to make known the mystery of the gospel, for which I am an ambassador in chains; that in it I may speak boldly, as I ought to speak" (Ephesians 6:18–20).

The apostle Peter, who preached the great sermon on the day of Pentecost that resulted in three thousand souls being added to the kingdom, was later arrested with John for healing a lame man. He and John were thrown into prison overnight, grilled by the religious leaders of the city the next day, and then released with a stern warning never to preach about Jesus again. When their fellow believers heard all this, they prayed for Peter and John, "Now, Lord, look on their threats, and grant to Your servants that with all boldness they may speak Your word" (Acts 4:29). The Scriptures go on to say that after they had prayed, they were filled with the Holy Ghost, and they "spoke the word of God with boldness" (vs. 31).

Do you lack boldness today in sharing Jesus Christ with others? Ask God to give you boldness.

## Boldness Born of Love

In his first letter to the church, the apostle John says, "Love has been perfected among us in this: that we may have boldness in the day of judgment; because as He is, so are we in this world. There is no fear in love; but perfect love casts out fear, because fear involves torment. But he who fears has not been made perfect in love" (1 John 4:17–18).

Your lack of boldness is very likely related to a lack of love for others.

Most of us don't like to face that fact. We like to see ourselves as being loving, generous-hearted, willing-to-sacrifice-for-others people. The truth is that most of us are still looking out for number-one: ourselves.

We're more concerned about what other people will think of us than about how the Lord desires to love other people through us.

Ask the Lord to give you a renewed, dynamic, deep, and compassionate love for other people. Make it your desire to love people as Jesus loved them.

## Loving Is an Act of the Will

Love is far more than emotion. It is an act of your will. It is choosing to love and choosing to pray, "Lord, give me more of Your love for the men and women I encounter as I walk life's paths."

Love is also the foremost characteristic that is given to us by the Holy Spirit, as Romans 5:5 declares, "Because the love of

God has been poured out in our hearts by the Holy Spirit who was given to us."

The Bible defines the very nature of God as being one of love (See 1 John 4:8). Growing in your love for others is really allowing more of the love of Jesus Christ to be manifested in your life. It is receiving God's love in such a way that it overflows.

Stop to consider what it really means to you to be saved. Consider what your destiny would be if you did not know the Lord; ponder the fact of everlasting separation from your Heavenly Father and eternal death. Try to imagine what your life would be like if you didn't know Jesus Christ as your personal Savior—what it would be like if you had no means of forgiveness and no Holy Spirit from which to draw wisdom, counsel, and help.

That is the fate, that is the existence, of those who have not received the Lord into their lives.

Will you allow the love of Jesus to flow through you to them, and in doing so, to conquer all your fear of rejection or ridicule?

Did you know . . .

## You *Can* Feel Like Witnessing to Others

Many people readily admit, "I have a hard time motivating myself to talk about Jesus to other people."

Very often that's because they are approaching the idea of sharing the Lord with themselves rather than with the other person.

They are more concerned about their own reputations than about the eternal spiritual fate and current human condition of the other person.

They are more concerned about what they are going to say or do than about what the other person needs to hear or receive.

They are more concerned about being rejected than about the other person's feelings of dejection.

They are more concerned about who they are than about who that other person might become in Christ Jesus.

The key to becoming motivated to share Christ is to see other people as Christ sees them. In other words, we must begin to see with His eyes.

## Begin to See Other People as They Really Are

I challenge you to conduct your own personal survey of humanity during the next week, and especially during the next twenty-four hours.

Look into the faces of people as they stand waiting for a bus or subway train. Look into the faces of people as they sit in an airport waiting lounge or a hotel lobby. Watch the faces of those you see in a local cafe or restaurant.

What a miserable lot you'll see!

Very seldom will you see someone who has a pleasant expression on her face, much less a smile. Most of the faces convey worry, sadness, despair, exhaustion, anger, fear, or just plain ol' trouble.

The Scriptures tell us again and again that Jesus was moved with compassion as He saw the multitudes. Note the phrase, "when He saw." (See Matthew 9:36 and 14:14 as examples.)

I have a very strong belief that we begin to feel compassion for others when we begin to see them as they truly are. In other words, seeing is a prerequisite for compassion.

Look into the eyes of people as you encounter them walking along a busy sidewalk. Look into the eyes of clerks as they wait on you. Look into the eyes of waiters or waitresses as they take your order. Nine times out of ten you will *not* see joy in their eyes.

Start seeing the people around you with new eyes today. If Christ is truly dwelling within you, you'll feel compassion beginning to move within you.

Ask the Lord Jesus to help you with this. Pray:

*Heavenly Father, I ask You today to help me see others as you see them. Help me to see their hurt, and to feel it, to the point where I will want to do something about it. I pray this in the name of Jesus. Amen.*

Beyond the hurdles of "lack of time" and "timidity" is one common to many people . . .

## The Hurdle of Anticipated Failure

I had a person say to me one time, "I'm not a strong enough Christian to share the gospel with someone." In essence, he was expecting to fail at the task before he had ever opened his mouth.

I've thought about that, and I've concluded that there really aren't any strong Christians—only a strong Christ. He's willing to work through anyone who will let Him. The apostle Paul continually pointed to his own personal weakness and affirmed that the strength he had was that of Christ working in and through him. Surely the same holds true for us.

Are there great men and women of God?

The greater likelihood is that there is a great God who is allowed to work through certain men and women.

Sometimes I meet people who think their past failures or reputations will get in the way of their witness. I can't think of anything in anyone's past that would disqualify them to talk about the Lord who has redeemed their past.

Don't let a past failure, mistake, or error be held up to you by the enemy of your soul as something that prohibits your telling another person about Jesus Christ. What the Lord has done in your heart to save you, deliver you, or heal you from that circumstance, addiction, instance, or relationship is what really matters. Focus on what *He* has done.

There's also a hurdle of "insufficiency" or "lack of ability" that some people put in their path. They don't feel that they are worthy to express the gospel. In fact, they aren't. None of us is! But Jesus is worthy to be expressed! He is the good news. We're not the focus of the supernatural news report, we're simply the reporters. We're not the star of this divine movie, we're the publicists. We're not the manufacturer of grace, we're the advertisers to let people know it's available.

The Scriptures say that we are "sufficient as ministers of

the new covenant [New Testament]" (2 Corinthians 3:6). You *are* capable!

One more hurdle in the path of some Christians is the "someday I'll" hurdle. It's the hurdle of good intentions. Let me assure you, however, that good intentions haven't yet led a soul to the Lord!

## The Hurdle of Good Intentions

Don't relegate your witness to something that will happen in the future . . .

- "When I'm strong enough in the Lord,"
- "When I overcome this trial,"
- "When I'm good enough to be His witness,"
- "When I've grown enough in the faith,"
- "When I've learned enough of the Bible," or,
- "When I've been a member of the church longer."

There's no prerequisite of training, time, experience, knowledge, membership, or accomplishment to be an active soul winner.

There's only the desire to see lost, hurting, and defeated people experience what you have experienced in the Lord.

Finally, there's the biggest hurdle of all—at least it's the one that I see the most people grappling with . . .

## The Hurdle of Fear

I recently read an article in which the author had conducted a study that revealed ninety percent of all fears have no basis in reality. Fear grips the mind. It torments. It restricts and binds. It causes us to limit what we do and say for the Lord.

When I ask people why they aren't more free in sharing the name of Jesus with those they perceive to be lost or in need, they nearly always tell me, "Fear, I guess."

When I probe further, I find that the fear is usually a fear of rejection or a fear of ridicule.

To my knowledge, nobody ever died of either ailment.

The consequence of your not speaking, however, may be a very real eternal death for the person who is never given the opportunity to receive Jesus Christ into his life.

This kind of fear—which is really rooted in pride, although we don't like to admit it—is a fear that comes from the enemy of our souls. It has nothing to do with an awe of God or the normal, instinctual fear of life-threatening situations. Fear of rejection and fear of ridicule are fears that do one thing in the lives of witnesses: keep them silent about the things of the Lord.

The enemy knows that if we refuse to share the love of God and the good news of salvation with others, his work is more than half done without any effort on his part.

Face up to the fears that you feel about bringing up the name of Jesus in a conversation. Say as Queen Esther said, "If I perish, I perish" (Esther 4:16). The alternative was for all of Esther's people to be annihilated.

Confront the reality head on . . .

# You Won't Lead the Whole World to Christ

Settle it in your mind at the outset that you will not lead the whole world to Christ. In fact, Jesus Himself said, "Broad is the way that leads to destruction, and there are many who go in by it. Because narrow is the gate and difficult is the way which leads to life, and there are few who find it" (Matthew 7:13–14).

Don't be discouraged that the odds are against you as you set out to tell others about the Lord. The vast majority of people don't know Him. Indeed, the vast majority of people may never know Him.

Your job and my job is to give an opportunity to those who *do* desire to know Him.

The world rejected Jesus. You will encounter those who reject you.

The world ridiculed Jesus. You will encounter a few who will openly ridicule you (although they are a very, very small percentage of the population).

The world misunderstood Jesus. You will encounter many people who misunderstand you—perhaps even some in your own church or family!

The world persecuted Jesus. You may feel persecuted, too, at times.

Jesus has a good word for you when you experience persecution:

> Blessed are those who are persecuted for righteousness' sake, /
> For theirs is the kingdom of heaven. Blessed are you when they
> revile and persecute you, and say all kinds of evil against you
> falsely for My sake. Rejoice and be exceedingly glad, for great is
> your reward in heaven, for so they persecuted the prophets who
> were before you *(Matthew 5:10–12)*.

## The Good News About Hurdles

The good news about these hurdles that we put in our paths is that the Holy Spirit can help us soar over them if we'll only ask for His help and then receive His help by faith and open our mouths.

The bad news about these hurdles is that none of them is a good excuse before the Lord for failing to tell others about Him.

Regardless of our excuses, we each have . . .

## A Three-fold Responsibility
## to the Kingdom

I believe very strongly that we have a three-fold responsibility to the kingdom of God. Jesus taught, "Seek first the kingdom of God and His righteousness, and all these things shall be added to you" (Matthew 6:33).

What do you seek in the kingdom of God? First, make certain that your own relationship with the Lord is growing and on target. Prayer and Bible reading are keys in this area. Make certain that you personally are in the kingdom.

Second, make certain that your relationships with fellow Christians are not marked by sin but are growing by Christ's love. Church involvement, family devotional times, and honest one-to-one encounters with other believers are crucial in building up a strong body of believers. Make certain that you are part of a group of people who are in the kingdom.

Third, seek to expand the kingdom by sharing the Word of God with those who are not yet a part of it.

Jesus, Himself, had this three-fold concern. He knew who He was in the Father. He knew His relationship to Almighty God.

He surrounded Himself with twelve men who were called to associate closely with Him and to share a deep faith-centered relationship. The relationship was one in which each person was destined not only to be part of a spiritual community but also to "go out." The word *apostle* literally means "sent one." Jesus didn't form a clique. He formed a missions team. The role of the followers of Jesus was to build a community that was ever expanding.

And yet, we so often preoccupy ourselves with various activities and social reforms without seeing those things as a means of winning souls.

For some of us, a concern for soul winning involves a resetting of our kingdom priorities to line up with God's priorities.

Finally . . .

## Recognize that Active Soul Winning Is the Greatest Thing You Can Do

Many of us dream of doing great things for the Lord. We'd like to have people recognize us as Christian leaders and perhaps even someday come to be regarded as saints. Even if we don't desire that other people recognize our godly qualities, we do hope for rewards in heaven.

One of the most haunting things I've ever read is this passage by my friend Dick Eastman in his book *The University of the Word:*

I saw the great King, seated upon His throne. On either side of the throne, I saw the great angels—Uriel, Raphael, Michael, and Gabriel. Before the throne stood another angel, the angel of the book. And by his side stood one of the mortals.

"Who is this that you have brought, and what are his claims?" asked the King.

"O King, this man was a great inventor who shed light on the pathways of man throughout the whole world."

"Then," said the King, "send him up and let him stand here by Uriel, the angel of light." So he went up.

And the angel brought another man before the throne. "Who is this and what are his claims?" asked the King. "This man was a great philosopher, who thought his thoughts after Thee," answered the angel.

And the King looked at him and said, "Send him up and let him stand here by the side of Raphael, the angel of reason." So he went up and stood by the side of Raphael.

And the angel brought a third mortal before the throne. "Who is this and what are his claims?" cried the King.

"This was a great patriot, who with his sword delivered his people out of the hands of tyrants," intoned the angel.

"Send him up, then, and let him stand by the side of Michael, the angel of the sword," responded the King. So he went up and stood by Michael.

And the fourth mortal came before the throne. "Who is this and what are his claims?" asked the King.

"This man sang holy songs, in praise of You, almighty King; songs which still echo through the Church of the Living God."

And the King said, "Send him up and let him stand and sing here by the side of Gabriel, the angel of song." And he did.

Then the angel brought another mortal before the throne. I wondered who he was and why he had been brought. In his person there was no note of greatness. His eyes contained no flash of genius. His face was beaten and torn by the trials of life. He was a simple, ordinary man. *Why,* I wondered, *has this man been called?*

And then the King spoke, "Who is this, and what are his claims?"

And the angel looked into the book, and lifting his head with a smile of joy, he shouted, "This man won a soul for Jesus Christ!"

And I never heard what the King on his throne said, for all of heaven rang with such a great shout, as angels and archangels, and cherubims and seraphims, and all the host of heaven, were singing, shouting, and rejoicing over that one soul that had been redeemed.

## You Have What It Takes

You don't need to be a scholar in order to be a soul winner.

You don't need to be a preacher.

You don't need to be ordained as a pastor.

You don't need to have a degree in Bible or even have completed a Bible training course.

You don't need to be a church member for many years.

You don't need to be a great public speaker.

All you need is to be willing to open your mouth and let the love of Jesus pour out of your heart toward another person and say to them, "Jesus loves you. He died for you so that when you believe in Him, He can forgive you of your sins and give you eternal life. Will you receive Him into your life as your Savior and Lord?"

No, it doesn't take *skill* to be a soul winner. It takes a desire to share Jesus with lost human beings.

# FIVE

# MAKING AN APPROACH

Much of what we have discussed thus far has probably been familiar to you. I hope that's true!

As we move into the area of technique, I'd like to raise a warning flag. It's very easy to fall into a pattern of doing things that relies only on human ability and memory, and therefore, to fail to recognize that our efforts at soul winning must be within the flow of the Holy Spirit's work in the world. For example, it's very easy to move from spiritually praying, "Lord, help me and guide me," to mentally saying, "I think I'll move on to step number three and see what happens." Techniques can become a substitute for spiritual sensitivity. I hope you will be aware of that as you read the remaining chapters of this book.

- Don't get ahead of the Holy Spirit as you converse with someone about the Lord.
- Don't be more concerned about getting through your presentation than you are with helping another person make a life-changing, eternity-determining decision.
- Don't allow salvation techniques to overshadow the Savior.

A relationship with the Lord Jesus is a spiritual matter. Soul winning techniques should always flow from that relationship, not be isolated as a pattern to follow with "one size fits all" as its motto.

Given that warning at the outset of this chapter, here are

some practical suggestions for approaching a person with an intent of sharing the gospel.

## Only Those Within Hearing Distance

When I find myself in a large room of hurting people, I have a deep desire within me to share Jesus Christ. Perhaps it's something about "seeing the multitudes." Perhaps it's an awareness that so many people in any identifiable group of people do not know the Lord in a personal, life-changing way. Of course, I don't want to share Him with every person I see—only those within hearing distance. Or in some cases, it's "overhearing distance."

Begin to share Christ with a person in a crowded room and you'll definitely see the "E. F. Hutton" effect take hold. People all around will be craning their necks to hear more of what you are saying.

If they don't know the Lord, they'll be straining out of curiosity—in fact, it might be a curiosity they don't even understand themselves. People are looking for something to satiate their inner hunger for the Lord, even if they don't know how to describe that unsettled feeling inside themselves.

On the other hand, some people will try to run away from what you are saying. Your words about the Lord Jesus will make them so uncomfortable they'll move away from you as fast as they can. While the Lord may be in hot pursuit of their souls, you can be assured that they are not yet ready to receive Christ as their own Savior. Let them leave and wish them Godspeed. Know that you have been just one more touch of the Holy Spirit in their lives as the Spirit woos them to Himself.

If a person overhearing your witness does know the Lord, he'll usually strain to hear whether what he thinks he is hearing is actually what he is hearing. He'll be delighted and overjoyed to hear a fellow believer sharing Christ with someone. Chances are, his own conversation with others will take a turn toward the Lord Jesus.

And always bear in mind that your approach will ultimately be to one person or perhaps two people who are traveling together.

## Where Do You Find the People?

Find people in any public place. I've found that I am frequently encountering several categories of people as I travel.

Waitresses.

Cab drivers.

Bellhops.

Hotel maids.

When you travel a great deal, you are around these people continually. Every major city has literally thousands upon thousands of people working in the four professions named above. Surely God can intersect your travel path with several who are ready to meet Him.

My work at a university now means that I have regular daily encounters with students, teachers, and staff members.

In your profession, you'll no doubt be in regular contact with still other categories of people, such as . . .

Airline passengers.

Subway passengers.

Shoppers.

Clerks.

Indeed, your profession, especially if it's a service profession, will put you in touch with

Clients.

Vendors.

Customers.

Manufacturing personnel.

If you work for a large organization, you're likely to encounter dozens of co-workers in any given day.

The opportunities are virtually endless!

## Be a Sensitive Observer

Watch people. See how they act and react. Watch their movements and the expressions on their faces.

Notice what kinds of books, magazines, or newspapers they are reading.

Ask the Lord as you do to show you something about a person as you watch the person in motion.

You can tell a great deal about a person just by watching him. Most emotions—such as sadness, dismay, pain, fear, distrust, defeat, sorrow, worry, pent-up anger, and grief—are readily portrayed in a person's physical demeanor.

Become a student of human behavior. Learn to recognize downcast eyes, hunched over shoulders, furrowed brows, clenched hands (or handbags or rolled up magazines), involuntary grimaces, and other facial and physical expressions for what they are—indicators of how a person is feeling on the inside.

## Reading a Person's Face

Most of us don't hide our emotions very well. Frustration and worry and sorrow are three strong emotions most people just can't hide.

When you see a person who is struggling with deep emotions, you may want to ask, "You've been experiencing some troubles in your life, haven't you?"

Some people respond, "How did you know?" or "Why do you say that?" I'm honest with them: "I just seemed to sense it. I may be wrong, but if I'm right, I'd like to help you if I can. Everybody needs a listening ear from time to time."

Other people will unburden their souls with no further invitation: "You wouldn't believe what I've been through lately" or, "You're right. I've certainly had my share of troubles lately."

A few may even start to cry or become too choked up for words.

A person who is in need—no matter what the cause or nature of the problem—is nearly always a person who is ready to hear the encouraging word that Jesus Christ died so that he might be forgiven, rise with Him in newness of life, and experience joy and peace.

The greatest antidotes in the world for trouble are joy and peace. Jesus promised to give us both.

Peace I leave with you, My peace I give to you; not as the world gives do I give to you. Let not your heart be troubled, neither let it be afraid (John 14:27).

These things have I spoken to you, that My joy may remain in you, and that your joy may be full (John 15:11).

Your sorrow will be turned into joy (John 16:20).

# Be Confident—and Show it!

Perhaps the most important thing you can do as you move through this world is to radiate the confidence of your own salvation. In my opinion, Christians should be the most confident people in the world.

Our confidence as Christians isn't in our own abilities. Our confidence is in the Lord. Our confidence rests in what He prompts us to do and say.

Our confidence is in knowing that Jesus Christ is our Savior, our sins are forgiven, we were created to bring glory to the Lord, we were created to have dominion over the earth, and we are bound for eternal life.

Confidence born of that knowledge is true confidence! And most people are looking for someone who knows what she believes and who can state what she believes with confidence.

# Confidence Attracts

If you portray a lack of confidence in what you are saying about Jesus, the person is likely to tune you out—because of your attitude rather than because of the words you are using. Confidence, however, attracts. It compels people who are seeking for the Lord to want to hear more of what you have to say about Him.

I had a man tell me in tears one day, "I've never had anybody talk to me like that. Thank you."

Another man said, "I've never talked with someone who has spoken to me with such peace and authority combined. It makes you really believable to me."

I took both of those statements as real compliments about the Lord's working through me. I certainly recognize it as His work and not something I've acquired as a skill or unique ability. Jesus spoke that way when He walked on this earth. He was a gentle and peaceful person in the way He dealt with those who were sick, hurting, doubting, suffering, or bruised by society or the religious leaders of that day. He came in a spirit of binding up the broken hearted and speaking good news to those with impoverished spirits. That's peace! And yet, He had authority over all principalities and powers. He walked and healed and spoke with great power. The combination is irresistible.

Again, it's His work in us and through us. Jesus even said about Himself in His humanity, "I don't do anything on my own. I do what the Father is telling me and empowering me to do." (See John 5:19.) The same is true for us. We are to speak and do what our Father is prompting us to speak and do through the power of His Holy Spirit at work in our lives.

## Be a Speaker of Friendly Words

The usual approach I take with people is that I seek to be friendly. Most people will respond to genuine friendliness with friendliness. I seek out opportunities by looking at people's eyes. If I get eye contact with someone, I smile at him and give a word of greeting.

Sometimes that alone opens up a conversation. The other person may well ask, "Are you from around here? Are you visiting?" At other times, I initiate a conversation.

I always try to get the person's name. In areas of public service (such as with waitresses or taxi drivers), the name of the person is usually displayed on a name badge or license. In beginning a conversation with a person, I use his name and then ask a question in a friendly manner.

I often ask as I meet people from various cities, "Are you

from around here?" If they are, I ask them to tell me something about their city, and especially, to tell me if there's anything encouraging happening in the area.

People frequently ask me, as I ask them, "What do you do?" The question usually refers to an occupation, but I've found it far more effective to give a reply that indicates my role—my job, my function—within the kingdom of God.

I reply, "I'm a teacher. I teach people how to live a fuller life and how to find God's plan for their lives." Their responses give me an immediate indication as to where they are in their relationship with the Lord.

"Making an approach" is really nothing more than initiating a friendly conversation in what is, for the most part, an unfriendly world.

It's taking time to notice another person.

It's making contact.

It's speaking friendly words in a friendly tone of voice.

When you stop to think about it, that's a good witness for the Lord in and of itself! The challenge now is to turn that friendly conversation into an opportunity for a life-changing encounter.

# SIX

# TURNING A CONVERSATION TOWARD THE GOSPEL

Recently, I was sharing a meal with three friends in a restaurant, and on one of the trips our waitress made to our table, I said to her, "We've got some very encouraging news to share with you, if you can come back by our table a little later when you aren't so busy."

She told us her shift was about over and that she'd stop by later. Sure enough, as we ended our meal, she came by and said, "Well, here I am."

I said, "Something very exciting has happened to all four of us."

She said, "All at the same time?"

I said, "No, all at different times, but the same thing."

She said, "What is it?"

I said, "We've all come to discover our need for the Lord Jesus Christ—that He died for our sins, and He arose from the dead, and that He desires to come into each one of our hearts and make us each a new person and give us peace of mind and joy and eternal life. He has made us each a new creation. Have you been longing for a change in your life?"

She said simply, "Yes, I have."

"Do you realize that the Lord Jesus is who you need?"

She said, "Yes." And we had the privilege of leading her in a prayer right there.

No sooner had we ended our prayer and were rejoicing together at her new-found life in Christ Jesus than her relief waitress came to our table, and I said to her, "Bobbie, you might be interested in knowing that Suzanne just accepted the Lord Jesus into her heart. She's been made a new creation, and you can probably tell by her smile and the look in her eyes that she has a newfound joy inside that comes from being forgiven of her sins. You need the same thing, don't you?"

She said, "Yes, I do." And we had the opportunity to lead her in a prayer, too.

## So Quickly? So Easily?

I don't always bring up the name of Jesus this quickly or easily, but the Lord has been teaching me some things lately about Himself and how He desires to work in the lives of lost men and women. These three principles have begun to ring true for me:

- The extension of an opportunity for a person to receive the Lord into his life need not be long or drawn out. Most of our soul winning conversations are far too long.
- More people are ready to receive and confess the Lord Jesus as their Savior than most of us have thought. This may be related to the difficult times we live in or to the spirit of revival that seems to be sweeping the world. It may also be that the Holy Spirit is answering my prayer and those of others that laborers will be sent into the harvest and that their paths will be directed to those who are ready to receive the Lord.
- People can receive the Lord anywhere and at any time. Alone or in a crowd. In motion or standing still. In any posture. Using a wide variety of words and phrases. The Lord sees the intent of the heart.

Through the years, I've settled on several questions that seem to work best for me in bringing a person to make a decision for the Lord. Again, I share them with you with a word of caution. The important aspect of any active soul winning conversation is to follow the leading of the Holy Spirit as He uses you, a unique individual, to share the news of His Son with another unique individual. Every encounter has distinctive qualities to it.

## "Is Anything Encouraging Happening?"

One of my favorite questions to ask is this: "Is anything encouraging happening in your life?" Or, "Do you see anything encouraging happening around you or in the lives of people you know?"

I ask these questions as if I'm conducting my own personal survey.

If the person responds negatively, I generally follow up by saying, "Well, there are encouraging things happening, and the most encouraging thing that is happening is that people are discovering their need for the Lord Jesus Christ and that life really isn't worth living without Him. They're receiving the Lord Jesus into their hearts and becoming new creations who have the peace of God. Do you know anyone that this has happened to, or has this perhaps happened to you?"

By starting with the more general statement, I find that most of the people with whom I speak remain very open.

Sometimes I rephrase that question so it becomes a statement. For example, let's imagine for a moment that you and I are sitting in a waiting room. I might turn to a person sitting near us and say, "Would you mind if my friend, here, shared with you for just a minute the most exciting thing that's ever happened to him?"

From my experience, I've found that most people will respond by saying "OK" or "sure, go ahead." Most people would like to hear a little exciting news.

Those who respond negatively generally are busy doing something—reading or working, for example—and are not the people to ask in the first place. Ask a person who isn't talking, reading, writing, doing handwork, and so forth. Look around. Many people in a waiting room are often just waiting.

An opening remark such as this lets the person know immediately that you are a positive person and that the conversation is going to be uplifting.

Another favorite question of mine is this:

## "Have You Noticed Any Signs of Spiritual Awakening in Your City?"

Many times a person will respond, "What do you mean?"

"Well, have you noticed that people seem more frustrated or dissatisfied with life, and that they are becoming more aware that they need something or someone outside themselves to bring peace into their lives?"

The person might respond, "Yes, I see people more frustrated and dissatisfied."

"That's often the way God begins to work with people as He shows them that God has made a way for them to have a personal relationship with Him. Through Christ's death on the cross, He's made a way for them to know Him and to receive the peace that only God can give."

If there's any sign of responsiveness, I go ahead to share the gospel more fully with the person.

A third favorite question of mine for turning a conversation to the Lord is this:

## "Have You Been Thinking More About the Lord Lately?"

"You mean you make that statement as the first thing you say?" one person said to me with a little shock in his voice.

Yes.

It doesn't really take long for a conversation to get to the heart of the gospel if you know where you're headed. If you are seeking to win souls and to give people an opportunity to receive Christ, then your conversation has a focus and a direction even before you make your opening remark. You frequently can move quickly and directly to key comments and questions.

The more I've shared Christ with people through the years, the more I've come to realize that *it doesn't take a long conversation to get to the root of a person's spiritual life.*

"Well," you may say, "that seems fairly abrupt."

Yes, it is a fairly abrupt approach. And yet, the majority of people I've talked with have this reaction to such a direct question:

- If they are ready to receive Christ, they are grateful that the conversation has taken that turn.
- If they have questions or concerns about Christ, such a question gives them an opportunity to voice those questions.
- If they are not ready to accept Christ, they will end the conversation quickly and you can move on.

Even if the person doesn't receive Christ, the direct simplicity of your question is likely to have a far greater impact on his life as he thinks about Christ and weighs the issue of his own spirituality in the coming days and weeks. It's more difficult to forget a direct, simple question than a long, veiled, never-to-the-point conversation.

I sometimes phrase this question more as a statement: "You've been thinking more about the Lord lately, haven't you?"

You might say, "Well, you're being a bit presumptuous, aren't you?"

Yes, if by presumptuous you mean that I'm presuming that the Holy Spirit has led me to that person for a purpose.

You see, I always assume at the outset of a conversation that the Holy Spirit's desire is for me to speak the name of Jesus to other people and to share something of the good news of Christ Jesus with them.

I can't think of a time when I met a person and the Holy Spirit whispered in my heart, "Don't bring up the name of Jesus."

You may say, "But what if I just think it's the Lord and it really isn't?" If you are operating in your own power and strength and claiming that your actions are of God, the Lord will deal with you about that. You'll be convicted about it. And if you persist in those actions, the Spirit will deal with you very directly about it. Chances are, however, if you are desiring to be a sincere witness for the Lord and are seeking to follow the leading of the Lord, you won't have that problem. Your problem is more likely to be one of timidity and speaking with "fear and trembling" rather than overconfidence and pride in self-generated ideas and words.

I believe with all my heart that the Holy Spirit desires that all of our conversations have a touch of Jesus in them and that all our thoughts and conversations should be sprinkled heavily with His name, His purposes, His concerns, His life, and His life-giving power.

Therefore, if it is the Holy Spirit's desire that even a seemingly casual conversation with a stranger should in some way be honoring to the Lord God, then I believe I'm correct in presuming that Jesus should be introduced into a conversation.

Furthermore, since I am intentionally seeking to be led by the Holy Spirit, since I have prayed in advance that the Holy Spirit would lead me in His paths and guide my steps that day, and since I've prayed for opportunities to speak to people about the Lord and to lead people to Christ, why *not* make the presumption that the person with whom I've made eye contact and shared a smile and a hello is someone with a heart already prepared by the Holy Spirit for the very conversation we are about to have?

The worst that can happen is that the person will say, "No, not really." (And yet, even that much of a conversation can cause the person to think about Christ so that the next time she is asked, "You've been thinking about the Lord more lately, haven't you?" she will respond affirmatively!)

The best that can happen is that within a matter of a few minutes, someone will be born anew in his spirit and become a newborn babe in Christ Jesus!

## An Excellent Barometer

The question, "You've been thinking more about the Lord lately?" actually provides an excellent means of determining very quickly where a person is in his relationship with the Lord God.

Frequently, a person will respond with something like:

- "Come to think of it, I have been watching a lot of Christian television lately."
- Or, "Yeah, my wife has been encouraging me a lot lately to go to church with her."
- Or, "Yes, I have."

Sometimes the person will proceed to tell me about specific problems or circumstances in his life that have been prompting a greater concern for spiritual matters.

In nearly all of those cases, I'm able to provide a word of spiritual encouragement or to speak to the person further about the saving power of Jesus.

I recently said to a waitress, "You've been thinking about the Lord in just the last couple of days, haven't you?"

She said, "It's very strange that you should ask me that. Last night I looked in the mirror and thought, *Lord, what's going on?*"

I said, "The reason you had that thought last night is that the Lord knew you've been thinking more about Him lately, and He knew I was going to be here today and I was going to ask you that question. Today is the day of salvation for you, and it's time for you to respond to the grace of God. Right now, you can bow your head and say, 'Lord Jesus Christ, I know I need you. Have mercy upon me, a sinner, and save my soul.' You're ready right now, so go ahead."

She bowed her head right there at the side of the table and said those words and received Christ into her life. A radiance flooded her face. She had come to the table to pour me a second cup of coffee. She left a new creature in Christ.

# A 90 Percent Chance for a Christ-Centered Conversation

By the way, I've found that of the people I ask this question, 90 percent respond to me, "Yes."

Are you surprised?

A lot of Christians are when I give them that statistic.

The fact is, people in our world today are thinking a great deal about the Lord—perhaps more so than ever before. Most people are surrounded by problems they can't solve. They are concerned about losing (or keeping) their jobs, about losing (or maintaining) their families, about losing (or keeping) their possessions, about losing (or keeping) control over their lives in a world that seems to be spinning out of control. The greater the fear and frustration and concern people have about the outer aspects of their lives, the more tender they seem to be toward God and the more they question the meaning of life, the purpose for their existence on this earth, and the way to find lasting inner peace.

Those who are without Christ know intuitively that something is missing in their lives. They know they are living with a degree of misery that's always present. Yes, most people are searching, to some degree or other, for a spiritual reality they can count on.

I believe with all my heart that if you will sincerely pray at the start of your day,

*Heavenly Father, use me today. Lead me to people with whom I can share the good news of Your Son. Give me an opportunity to lift up Your name on the earth,*

that God will answer your prayer! He will bring you into contact with those who are ready to hear about Jesus Christ. And you, too, can ask the question—"You've been thinking more about the Lord lately, haven't you?"—and have a ninety percent chance of entering into a conversation in which you share about the Lord Jesus and what He can mean to the other person.

Sometimes the person to whom you speak will be a Christian who is going through a difficult time. In those cases, this question opens up a direct opportunity for you to encourage a fellow brother or sister in Christ.

Sometimes the person to whom you speak will be someone who once had a relationship with Jesus but has allowed that relationship to grow stale, cold, or estranged. Your question opens the door for that person to renew their commitment to the Lord and enter again into the fullness of a warm, intimate relationship with Him.

The Lord seems to delight in putting the right people in just the right place for you to talk to!

## Responding to the Person's Pain

At other times, I don't ask a question at all, but rather, I respond to what I perceive to be the emotions being registered by the person.

You can usually tell what is inside a person by reading his face and especially by looking into his eyes.

I especially like to ask people who have a happy expression, "What's the reason behind that smile you have on your face?" or, "What's the cause for that smile I see in your eyes?"

If the person is a Christian and they readily know that Jesus is the reason for the glow in their eyes or the shine on their face, the question gives them a good opportunity to say a word about the Lord. (It gives them a little practice—a good thing for any member of the body of Christ to have!)

If the person gives a reason other than Christ as the reason for his or her smile, you can quickly take one of two approaches:

- "That's just great. Are you aware that this good thing that's happened to you is a gift from the Lord? The Bible tells us that every good and perfect gift comes from God. I'm thrilled that the Lord is doing this for you as an expression of His love." If the person makes any response at all to what you have said, you can proceed to share more fully with them your understanding of a good and loving Father who desires to express His love in and through each one of His children.
- "I'm happy for you! I've noticed that not many people have happy expressions on their faces, and it's always nice to meet someone who does. I have a joy in my heart, and the reason for it is that the Lord has forgiven my sins. You know, there's tremendous joy that comes when you know that your sins are forgiven and you no longer need to carry around a load of guilt." Listen closely to the per-

son's response. If they show the slightest inclination to pursue this line of conversation, share more fully how you came to experience the joy you feel and how they can experience it, too!

## Speaking to the Pained or Doom-and-Gloom Person

When you see a person who seems to radiate pain or to embody the phrase, "doom and gloom," you might say . . .

- "You seem down. Is there something that, or someone who, is hurting you?" In this day when so much is being written and said about abuse, that question is not an intrusive or alien one. Listen closely to how the person answers your question. If he is being terrorized by someone, help in whatever practical ways you can. And conclude your suggestions by adding, "There's someone who would like to be your ally in this situation" and proceed to tell him about the Lord Jesus.
- "You seem to be having a bad day." The person will generally respond by agreeing with your assessment or by telling you a little of what's gone wrong. Rather than commiserate as a fellow sufferer, follow-up by saying, "I've found someone that makes each day go a little better for me." And proceed to tell him about your relationship with Jesus Christ and the difference He has made in your life.

I have a friend who uses this approach to open a conversation with a person . . .

## "Has Anyone Told You Today that God Loves You?"

If the person says yes (which is unlikely), he follows up, "Well, let me add my witness to theirs. God truly does love you." He might then ask him if he knows the Lord as his

Savior, or seek to encourage the person if he is already a Christian.

If the person says no, he has an open door to say, "Well, God *does* love you. In fact, He loves you so much that He sent His Son, Jesus, to die on the cross for your sins so that you can be forgiven and freed from guilt and have peace and joy in your life and live with the Lord forever in heaven."

This man leads many people to the Lord each year, nearly all of whom are introduced to the gospel in conversations that are opened with that very simple, non-confrontational, lovingly asked question.

Since I met this man and heard about his approach, I've used it on occasion and found that it works for me, too.

## Responding to What a Person Is Reading

I have a friend who began talking to the person next to him on an airplane and noticed his fellow passenger was reading an article about a tragic earthquake. He said, "Have you ever been in an earthquake?"

The other man said, "No, but my brother lives in California, and he has been in earthquakes."

He said, "I don't know how people get through difficult times like that without the Lord."

"Hmmmm," the other man said, more as a response than in agreement.

"Having the Lord in my life has made it possible for me to feel encouragement in my life no matter what the circumstances I'm facing. There's no better feeling than knowing that my sins are forgiven and that I have eternal life awaiting me on the other side of death. Have you received Jesus into your life so that you know your sins are forgiven?"

"No, I don't think I have—at least, not in the way you just said it."

"Well," my friend went on, "do you believe that Jesus is God's Son who came in the flesh?"

"Yes, I believe that."

"Do you believe that He died on the cross so that your sins might be forgiven?"

"Yes, I believe that, too."

"And that He rose again so you might have newness of life?"

"Yes."

"Then you're ready to receive Him into your life right now, aren't you? If you'd like, I can lead you in a prayer, and you can settle this issue once and for all right now."

The man put down his magazine and said, "OK," and they prayed a simple prayer together. His destination that day may have been an earthly one, but his destination for eternity was changed in that hour to heaven!

## Responding to Your Travel Destination

Actually, responding to a travel destination may also provide an opening to share Christ. Are you scheduled to fly into, or out of, Washington, D.C.? You might say to a fellow airline passenger, "I've been delighted to learn that a growing number of people in Washington are coming to an awareness of their need for the Lord."

You can then go on to share the names of some of those whom you know have spoken or written publicly about their relationship with the Lord—such as Senator Strom Thurmond of South Carolina, Senator Don Nickles of Oklahoma, former Congressman Mark Siljander of Michigan, and Vice-President Dan Quayle—and you might add, "Have you been made more aware recently of *your* need for the Lord?"

## Taking a Turn in a Political Conversation

If you find yourself involved in a conversation that relates to politicians, to the issue of separation of church and state, to the freedom of religion, or to any other issue related to Washington, D.C., the federal government, elected officials, or an upcoming congressional vote or election—try this as an opening line: "I was amazed recently to learn that many of our presidents have been strong supporters of the Bible."

If you aren't familiar with some of the statements that our

past presidents have made, I offer you these quotes as background:

> *It is impossible to account for the creation of the universe without the agency of a Supreme Being. And it is impossible to govern the universe without the aid of a Supreme Being.*
> —George Washington, first president of the United States

> *I have made it a practice every year for several years to read through the Bible.*
> —John Adams, second president of the United States

> *The Bible is the Rock on which our republic rests.*
> —Andrew Jackson, seventh president of the United States

> *Nothing but kind providence of our Heavenly Father could have saved me.*
> —John Tyler, tenth president of the United States

> *In regard to this great Book, I have but this to say: It is the best gift God has given to man. All the good the Savior gave to the world was communicated through this Book. Except for it, we would not know right from wrong. All things most desirable for man's welfare, here and hereafter, are to be found in it.*
> —Abraham Lincoln, sixteenth president of the United States

> *Hold fast to the Bible as the anchor of your liberty; write its precepts in your hearts and practice them in your lives.*
> —Ulysses S. Grant, eighteenth president of the United States

> *If a man is not familiar with the Bible, he has suffered the loss which he had better make all possible haste to correct.*
> —Theodore Roosevelt, twenty-sixth president of the United States

> *Inside the Bible's pages lie all the answers to all the problems man has ever known. I hope Americans will read and study the Bible. . . . It is my firm belief that the enduring values presented in its pages have a great meaning for each of us and for our nation. The Bible can touch our hearts, order our minds, and refresh our souls.*
> —Ronald Reagan, fortieth president of the United States.

Regardless of the person's response to your statement, you can proceed by saying, "I don't know everything there is to know about this issue of politics, but I do know what the Bible has meant to me. It has been the way I've learned about the Lord Jesus Christ. Do you know Him?"

# Letting Your Neighbors Know Where They Can Find a Christian

I have a friend who has made it a point down through the years to visit each new family that moves into her neighborhood and, in the course of a friendly neighborhood chat, to say, "You know, my husband and family and I are all Christians. We love the Lord Jesus and are very thankful that we have received Him into our lives. We each have a great peace, knowing that He has forgiven us of our sins and made us new on the inside, and we consider it a great joy and privilege to talk about Him, to share His Word, or to pray with anyone who wants to meet Him. If you'd ever like to meet the Lord, we'd be happy to introduce you to Him."

She recently shared with me, "Some have accepted the Lord. Others haven't. But I have the assurance that if anyone in our neighborhood desires to know the Lord, he knows where to find a Christian who can introduce him to Jesus."

# One Formula Doesn't Fit All

God is a creative God. He never does the same thing twice.

The same is true in the way He leads each of us to a greater understanding of Himself.

As you converse with people, be aware of their uniqueness. Catch a glimpse of how God has been working in their lives, and catch a glimpse of who they are. Ask the Holy Spirit to reveal to you a little of His plan and purpose for their lives.

Acknowledge their gifts and talents as coming from the Lord. Note the way they express themselves—in their dress, their words, their mannerisms. Their creativity is a gift from God.

Notice whether they have an accent. Where are they from? What is their background? What has led them to the place where you are encountering them?

Recognize that our heavenly Father has put them in specific jobs or careers or work situations and has surrounded them with unique relationships, all in His effort to prepare them to come to a full saving awareness of His Son, Jesus Christ.

- Don't work your "soul winning program." Explore their lives.
- Don't be so concerned about the next step on your soul winning agenda that you fail to appreciate who others are in the Lord.
- Don't be so worried about your own reputation that you lose sight of the ways in which the Lord has put you in touch with other people to help them in their need.

Each incident, each encounter, each conversation, each person, is distinctive.

At the same time, you'll no doubt find that certain phrases given to you by the Holy Spirit seem to work better than others in turning a unique, distinctive conversation toward Jesus.

## Discover What Fits You Best

Don't be afraid to try what works for another person. You'll discover quickly whether you are comfortable with an approach and whether it leads to conversations about the Lord that result in souls saved. You may try several approaches before you discover the one that works best for you. You may also find the Lord leading you to use one approach for a period of time, or in certain situations, and yet another approach during another season or in other circumstances of your life.

Avoid getting locked into any one method. Remember always that the Lord used many methods in His ministry. He approached each person as a distinctive individual even though the overall tenor and message of his ministry had great consistency.

Finally, one of my favorite approaches is to take on the role of . . .

## A Good-News Reporter

There's so much bad news coming at us from all sides, nearly every person appreciates a word of good news.

If you ask, "Say, would you like to hear a piece of good news?" nearly everybody will say, "Sure!"

I recently got into a cab in front of a hotel and said, "I've got a piece of good news!"

The driver said, "What is it?"

"That bell captain," I said, pointing out the man, "just asked the Lord Jesus Christ to come into his life, to forgive him of his sins, and to grant him eternal life. He just became a brand new creature in Christ and has a peace of heart and a joy that he's never experienced before. Isn't that great news?"

"Yeah," the cab driver said. "That *is* good news."

"Would you like to experience that, too? You can, you know."

The cab driver said, "How do you mean?" which I always interpret as an expression of interest in knowing more. All the way to my appointment, I shared with him what he needed to do to invite the Lord Jesus into his life. When we arrived at my destination, I asked him as I paid the fare, "Would you like to make that decision today?"

He said, "I'm not ready to do that right now, but I'll sure think about what you've said."

I responded, "Remember, you don't need anyone else around when you get ready to accept the Lord Jesus Christ as your Savior. You simply need to pray with a sincere heart, 'Lord, have mercy on me as a sinner. I receive You as my Savior. I ask You to forgive me of my sins and to come into my life and give me Your peace and joy.'" He nodded.

Even though we didn't pray together in that hour, I have a faith-born confidence in my heart that he has since found a time and place to pray that prayer. Furthermore, I have the knowledge that he knows where to turn to find another Christian since he frequently encounters the bell captain at the hotel from which he picked me up!

# Be a Johnny Appleseed for the Gospel

I admire Johnny Appleseed. Everywhere he went, he planted seeds. Many grew. Many didn't. The result of his life, however, was a trail of apple trees across several states, a legacy of his willingness to stoop down frequently to plant a seed. Johnny Appleseed didn't grow the trees. He didn't return to prune them. He didn't pick fruit from them. But they came to be because he planted the seeds in God's good earth and trusted God to bring forth trees.

Take on his attitude as you face tomorrow. Go from your home determined to tell others about Jesus, as if you are planting seeds. Trust God to bring forth trees that will be planted by the rivers of water. (See Psalm 1.)

# SEVEN

# ASSUMPTIONS TO MAKE AND NOT TO MAKE

Recent studies show that more than a billion people—one out of every four people living today—have never even heard the *name* of Jesus, much less that "it is appointed for men to die once, but after this the judgment" (Hebrews 9:27).

I thank God for every missionary, and I pray for missionary friends of mine daily. Yet, there are far too few missionaries to accomplish the task of evangelizing the world. In many nations, cultural barriers and governmental regulations severely limit, or prohibit altogether, the work of missionaries.

Two things can crash through these barriers to take the gospel into all nations—and into all homes within our own nation.

*First, the printed word.* You can take part in spreading the printed word in several ways:

- Support organizations that print the good news of God's love and distribute it in unreached parts of the world—in the form of Bibles, New Testaments, the Gospel of John, Bible teaching materials, or tracts.
- Carry tracts with you always, several kinds. Be quick to pass them out to those you encounter during a day.
- Leave tracks behind as you travel, especially in public places. (I especially recommend tracts in Spanish since it is the primary language of many people in large cities.)

*Second, personal witnessing.* It is virtually impossible to stop a personal conversation from taking place, no matter what the laws of a nation may be. And no one can stop the spread of the wildfire of God's love, once a match is lit to a ripened field.

As we approach people on an individual basis, we need to avoid making several assumptions about those who don't know the Lord. Let me share what I perceive several of these assumptions to be. First . . .

## Don't Assume that Everyone Has Heard

In the United States, it's easy to assume that people know the full and accurate truth about Jesus. An assumption that people *don't* know about Him is more accurate. In spite of the abundance of churches in our communities, the number of Bibles sold each year, and the number of gospel radio and television programs being aired, many many people—some of whom are very highly educated—don't know that Jesus came into this world and gave His life on a cruel cross so that they could be saved from eternal damnation and given eternal life.

Most people in our culture today, however, have heard the name of Jesus. Through watching a Christian television program, hearing a Christian radio broadcast, picking up a tract in a waiting room, or attending church once or twice in their lives with a friend, most people know that a man named Jesus lived and that He has something to do with Christianity.

Never assume, however, that a person in the United States of America knows more than that! Not even someone who tells you she is a member of a church.

Many of the people you encounter will have some degree of false information about Jesus. In my conversations with both churched and unchurched people, I've found that people frequently have more *incorrect* information about Jesus than they have correct information. Rather than try to undo the false information that a person has, put your emphasis on the *correct* information they need to have.

True, they might know about a baby born in a manger at Christmas. They might even know about a man named Jesus who lived on the earth nearly two thousand years ago. They might consider Him to have been a good teacher or a highly moral person. They may even know about the death of Jesus by Roman crucifixion on Good Friday, and they may even know that Easter Sunday is a celebration of the fact that Jesus rose from the dead.

Yet, they may not know that the baby Jesus who was born in the manger was born to die. They may not know that the words Jesus spoke then are life-giving to their souls today. They may not know that Jesus was more than just a good person, that He is the sacrifice for their sins and He paid the price of death so that they don't have to be separated from God and so that they can live with God for all eternity. They may not know that Jesus is the only way, the only truth, the only means to eternal life.

And unless they hear this life-changing good news, they can't believe on Him and receive Him into their lives.

Even those who tacitly and culturally call themselves "Christians" may not know the reality of John 3:16—that "God so loved the world, that he gave his only begotten Son, that whosoever believeth in him should not perish, but have everlasting life."

This, then, is the message that we must be prepared to whisper from ear to ear to ear.

## The Gospel Is a One Tells One Tells One Equation

The gospel message was never intended to be limited in its proclamation to an exclusive few within the church. From the very beginning, the gospel was spread by one person telling another person, that person telling yet another, and that person sharing with another as well.

Souls are added to the Kingdom one at a time. Decisions are made on an individual basis.

As I began to allow the Lord to work through me and became more bold in sharing His life within me with those around me, the Lord convinced me of something that I believe is true for all believers.

*It is the Lord's desire to reproduce what He is doing in your life in the lives of literally hundreds of other people.*

Don't leave it up to a radio preacher.

Don't leave it up to a television evangelist.

Don't leave it up to the missionaries.

Don't leave it up to a preacher who is holding a crusade or seminar or meeting in your city or church.

Don't leave it up to anybody but the person who looks back at you in the mirror. In summary . . .

## Don't Assume Somebody Else Will Do It

A few years ago, I had the privilege of attending an international convention of Christian leaders in our nation's capital. Literally thousands of Christians converged on that hotel conference center during a five-day period.

I began to ask several of the hotel workers, one by one, if they knew what the conference was all about. Several of them knew the topic of the conference and that Christian leaders were attending. Then I asked, "Has anybody shared with you how to become a Christian and receive the Lord Jesus into your life and experience His forgiveness of your sins and have the peace, joy, and eternal life that only Christ can give?" Nearly every person I asked said no.

I took that as my cue to share the gospel with the person and to give him an opportunity to receive the Lord. "You know," I'd close, "this conference may have been designed by the Lord just for you, so that you and I would have this opportunity to meet and talk about the Lord, and so that you could have the privilege of becoming a new creature in Christ Jesus today, right now." A number of people with whom I shared did receive Christ. A maid. A young security guard at the entrance to the exhibitors area. A hotel maintenance worker. And eight hotel security guards.

It was a good convention for the Lord's kingdom, quite apart from the scheduled program!

One man, already a Christian, told me that he had worked during this same convention for the past four years, and I was the first person to inquire about his soul.

I found that utterly amazing. Here were thousands of men and women supposedly convening to discuss ways in which to more effectively and efficiently spread the gospel, and they had overlooked the very people God had put in their paths. They were so busy talking to one another that they had forgotten to mention the name of the Lord to those who cleaned their rooms, carried their bags, waited on their tables, called their cabs, or provided them with other normal hotel and restaurant services.

Never assume that someone else in your church, at your convention, in your Bible study, in your Sunday school class, or in your particular Christian group will share the Lord with a person in your midst. Instead, assume that being an active soul winner is as much your responsibility as it is that of anyone else.

## Your Pastor May Not Even Be an Active Soul Winner

Don't assume that your pastor is an active soul winner.

Many Christians leave soul winning up to their pastors or other members of their church staffs. They believe either that it's a preacher's job to win souls or that the ordained clergy are the only ones qualified for the role.

Friend, it's the great commission of our Lord to *every* Christian to be a witness and to share the good news of the gospel with those who are lost.

In the first place, your pastor won't encounter all of the people you encounter and all the people everybody else in your church encounters. Most pastors spend virtually all of their time in direct ministry to people within the church—visiting the sick, calling on the homebound, counseling those in crisis times, conducting weddings and funerals, and dealing with dozens of administrative chores involved with the running of a church facility—not to mention the time they spend in prayer, Bible study, and sermon preparation.

In the second place, many pastors don't know how to win souls. Your pastor may be just as inexperienced in this area as you are, or more so!

I firmly believe the job of soul winning belongs first and foremost to lay people. We're the ones who go out fishing for souls, and we bring them to the pastor for nurturing and teaching of God's Word. We're the ones who are to invite lost souls to come with us to church, where the preacher can present the gospel to them in a sermon.

A second important assumption NOT to make is this . . .

# Don't Assume that Anyone Is Beyond the Need for Salvation

Romans 5:19 tells us, "For as by one man's disobedience many were made sinners, so by one Man's obedience many will be made righteous." We were each born with a sinful nature. Jesus came, however, to reverse that situation in our lives.

Sometimes we are reluctant to share about the Lord Jesus with those whom we perceive to be good people. You know the people I mean—they go to church, they live good moral lives, they don't break the law.

Our nature as sinners is not the result of something we do. It's the result of something we are. We're born with a sinful nature that needs redeeming. Have you ever noticed that nobody has to teach a child to lie? Nobody has to teach a child to cry "Mine!" or to give an emphatic "No!" to any hint of authority. Our sinful nature is a part of our inherited humanity. We each need to be redeemed from our basic nature.

## Two Opposites but One Lord

Don't assume that a person of one particular social class or economic status is in greater need of the Lord than another.

The Lord confirmed this truth to me in a very vivid way one day. A friend and I were walking through a park in a large city when we spotted a fellow with a beard and ragged clothes. He was hunting through the garbage can for food. We bought him a hot dog and an apple and sat down with him. He told us he had come to the city from North Carolina four years before to find a job, which never materialized. He had been on the streets most of the time since.

My friend and I shared with him, led him to the Lord, and urged him to get in touch with the Salvation Army. I heard from him later that he did go to the Salvation Army, that he did get a job, and that he is going on with the Lord.

That night I was having dinner with this same friend in a swank hotel restaurant and seated at the table next to us was a business woman who was attending a convention being held there. She had an ID tag pinned to her expensive, conservative suit and the label above her name said "Financial Planners."

We began to converse casually with her and she shared with us a little about her job as a financial advisor to major corporations. She was obviously affluent and savvy. Then, without our really seeking to turn the conversation in any direction, she began to relate the last time she had been in the hotel and all that had happened in the two years in between. She told of a traumatic divorce that had left her on the verge of suicide and how her son had ended up in a mental hospital.

Her life on the inside was every bit as raw and hurting as that of the man we had met earlier in the day at the park. With her, too, we prayed, and she received the Lord into her life.

Affluent or homeless. Both are without hope if they don't have the Lord.

## Don't Discount the Value of Any Soul

Very often we tend to look at a person and say, "Wow, wouldn't it be great if *that* person came to know the Lord."

The fact is, it's great when any person comes to the Lord.

A person may be a world-class athlete, a journalist, an actor, a business executive, an important government official, or even the leader of a nation . . . but if she doesn't know Jesus, she is just as lost as any other sinner.

A person may be a maid, a cab driver, a factory worker, a cook in a fast-food restaurant, or have no job at all—perhaps even no home at all—and if he does know Jesus, he is a child of God, a joint heir with Christ Jesus, bound for heaven.

God is no respecter of the outward accomplishments of a person, and He is not willing that any person should be lost for all eternity. He is equally concerned about each of us, regardless of our positions in life.

May we never forget that God loves all people—regardless of their culture, race, or creed. He sent His Son, Jesus Christ, to pay the penalty for sin for all people who will receive this free gift of salvation with a heart of faith.

## Don't Assume that a Person of Another Religion Is Unreachable

Sometimes we Christians tend to be intimidated if we hear a person say he is a Buddhist, a Hindu, a Muslim, a Jew, or perhaps a member of a sect or Eastern religious offshoot that we've heard nothing about.

Always bear in mind that no matter how entrenched people are in their worship of a false God or how limited their understanding is about Jesus Christ and His sacrifice for them on the cross, the fact does not change that Jesus died for their sins, that the Holy Spirit is working in their lives to bring them to an understanding and acceptance of Jesus as Christ, and that without the Lord Jesus Christ, there's a void in their lives that only He can fill.

I never argue religion with a person. In fact, I make it a point never to enter into an argument of any kind.

If a person tells me he is a Buddhist, for example, I do not respond negatively about Buddhism or attempt to point out the differences between their religion and Christianity. I simply say to him, "I have received the Lord Jesus Christ into my life. I'm very glad that I did, because my relationship with Him has given me a freedom from guilt and a joy and peace that I never had before. Jesus Christ has completely transformed my life on the inside and I believe He can do that for *any* person who will call upon Him and invite Him into his life." (Note that it only takes three sentences and about twenty seconds to share that much truth!)

In taking such an approach, I move the conversation off the subject of religion and on to the fact of a relationship with

Jesus Christ. Furthermore, I'm sharing personal experience. Nobody can argue with a personal testimony. You know what you know for yourself. And finally, I'm sharing in a very succinct way how a person might come to know the Lord for himself.

Spoken sincerely and with the love of the Lord for the other person, those words can be a powerful testimony that rings in the ears of the other person for a long time.

## Don't Assume Someone Is Too Brilliant for You to Approach

A number of years ago I had the privilege of leading a college chemistry professor to the Lord. Later, I was amazed to discover that no one had ever asked him before our encounter to accept the Lord. He had heard about the Lord, but he had never been asked to believe on Him or to receive Him into his life.

Don't be intimidated by a person with degrees after her name. Don't be intimidated by your doctor, dentist, attorney, or other professional advisor. Without the Lord, these people in your life may have a brilliant and successful future on earth, but they have no future—yet—in heaven.

Trust the Lord to use the words of the simple to confound the wise (as the apostle Paul taught). Trust the Lord to honor the "foolishness of preaching" (which is proclaiming the truth about the Lord). Trust the Lord to reveal to a person the sincerity of your heart and the truth of your words, quite apart from any appraisal of external reputation, appearance, or standing.

## Don't Assume Someone Is Too Powerful or Important for You to Approach

In the same manner, don't assume that someone is too powerful or important. Remember the centurion who came to Jesus asking humbly that He send only an "order" for the centurion's servant to be healed. Jesus said about this man's request that He had seen no greater faith in all of Israel!

I once had the opportunity to share the Lord with a high-ranking military official who occupied the seat next to me on a flight. I found his acceptance of the Lord very straight-forward, very much in keeping with his military background. Sometimes those in positions of authority understand how to receive "higher orders" very simply and obediently.

## Don't Assume the Person Whom You See Often Knows the Lord—Ask!

I work for a Christian university. So does the janitor who empties the trash in our offices and vacuums the floors. He has worked at the institution for years; I joined the administrative staff just a few months ago.

On evenings I worked late, I encountered this man for several weeks. We exchanged a little general conversation each time, and then one day as I was preparing to leave the office, I felt the Holy Spirit prompting me to ask this man, "Have you received the Lord Jesus into your life as your personal Savior?"

He said, "No, I haven't."

I said, "You'd like to have the peace of mind that comes from knowing that your sins are forgiven and that you have a relationship with the Lord, wouldn't you?"

He said simply, "Yes, I would."

I said, "Well, today is the day of salvation for you. You can receive the Lord into your life right now!"

We prayed there in my office, and he went on about his work and I went home. I couldn't help but wonder as I went, *How many years has this man waited for someone in this Christian institution to ask him if he'd like to receive the Lord?*

Now, each time I see this man, I try to find something encouraging to say to him in the Lord. I know where he's at, spiritually speaking, and know the Lord has put him across my path to help build him up in the faith.

Do you work for a church, a Christian school, a para-church or ministry organization, or some other company or organization that considers itself Christ-centered? Don't assume that everyone who works alongside you has received the Lord as his personal Savior. Find out where your co-workers are in the Lord. There's only one way to know for sure: ask them.

## Don't Assume the Person Is Unreachable Because He Doesn't Speak English

From time to time, the Holy Spirit has prompted me to approach someone who doesn't speak English or who speaks English as a second or third language. I've found that if the Holy Spirit is truly guiding the encounter, there's virtually always someone nearby who does speak both English and the language of the other person and who is willing to translate.

During the Olympics, I worked as part of an evangelism team, and one afternoon I encountered a woman who spoke no English but showed interest in what she perhaps perceived to be the love of the Lord in my general countenance. The woman who was with her seemed in a hurry. I asked, however, "Can you tell her in Spanish what I'm telling you in English?"

She agreed, and as she repeated phrase by phrase the simple explanation of the good news that I was giving her, both women began to receive the words the Lord was giving me into their spirits. As it turned out, the woman who was doing the translating was just as willing to receive the Lord as the one to whom I had initially been drawn. After we prayed together, their faces were aglow with the light of Jesus, and they kept saying over and over, "Gracias, gracias, gracias."

Even after I crossed the parking lot and looked back at them, they were still smiling and waving to me.

## Don't Assume You Must Have a Special Time or Place

The news that they could receive the Lord "any time and any place" was great news for Lorita and Shannon.

One evening a friend and I decided to stop in for a meal at a favorite Mexican restaurant of ours. Halfway through the meal, I asked the waitress, "Lorita, you're with the public all the time . . . have you noticed a hunger among people for more of God?"

"Yes," she said, "now that you mention it, I have."

My dinner companion and I shared with her about the three people we had met that morning who had become aware of their need for Christ, recognized He died on the cross to pay for their sins and rose again from the dead to live His life through them and to give them a new heart, and who had invited Christ to live within them.

Her eyes sparkled. "Has that ever happened to you, Lorita?"

"I go to church," she said.

"Yes, but have you ever made a personal decision to ask Christ into your heart? You want to do that, don't you?"

"You mean right here?"

"You can do it right where you are."

She prayed with me, and her face glowed as she moved on to another table to wait on a customer. At that moment, Shannon, the barmaid in the restaurant, walked by.

"Did you hear the good news?" I asked her.

She stopped in her tracks. "No . . . what?"

"Lorita just found peace with God."

"She did? What do you mean?"

"Yes, she accepted Christ into her heart as her personal Savior and Lord. Did you know you can have that same peace?"

"How?"

"By asking Christ into your heart."

"When? Where?"

"Now . . . right here."

Her eyes grew about as big as saucers. Through the years, I've found that many people look at me with wide-eyed awe when I tell them they can accept Jesus any place and at any time. They are so relieved that they don't need to go to a church or enter some type of lengthy catechism in order to invite Jesus into their lives. It's an absolute "wonderment" to them that they can receive Him right where they are. Shan-

non phrased her wonder in an unusual, fresh way. She said,
"You mean . . . you mean . . . I don't have to go through
religion?"

"That's right!"

Standing there in her red miniskirt and fishnet stockings,
balancing a tray of bottles and glasses, she repeated a short
prayer with us and gave us her name and address so we
could send her follow-up materials.

Finally . . .

## Don't Assume a "No" Once
## Is a "No" Always

Have you shared the good news of the Lord with someone
who then rejected your invitation to receive Christ? Do you
see that person often—or will you see him again?

Continue to share. You can always say, "Have you thought
any more about receiving the Lord into your life? He's still
waiting to give you forgiveness of sins, His peace and joy,
and the assurance of eternal life."

Without nagging, hounding, quarreling, or making a
scene, look for opportunities to share the Lord with the person each time you see him.

I have a friend who frequently says to her family members
who haven't received Christ into their lives: "I'm still praying
for you to receive all that the Lord Jesus has to give you. I still
want to live in heaven with you someday." No more needs to
be said to lift up the Lord!

# DISCERNING WHAT THE LORD IS DOING

Have you ever watched an expert shopper in the produce section of a grocery store?

She carefully sorts the fruit and vegetables displayed there, picking up this one and that one, discerning which product is ripe and at its prime.

The farmer goes through the same process at harvest—checking daily, sometimes even hourly—for the sugar content of a crop to reach the optimum level, for the maximum percentage of produce to be ripe, for the heads of grain to burst open.

Perhaps unfortunately, ripe souls—those who are ready to receive Jesus as their Savior—are not as easily discernible as market produce or agricultural crops.

## The Readiness Test for a Soul

The only way you know who is ready to receive the Lord into his life is to ask the question, "Would you like to receive Jesus as your Savior?"

On the surface, you can't tell who is ready and who isn't.

The Holy Spirit operates at a deep level in a person's life. The readiness of a person to accept Jesus as Christ cannot be seen in his dress, possessions, line of work, sex, age, or race. It is frequently not discernible by facial expressions, stress level, relationships, or even by behavior. Some of the most successful looking and acting people are miserable inside and are seeking a peace of heart that only the Lord can provide. Some of those who say and do all the right things in society are aching for an opportunity to find greater meaning in their lives. On the contrary, some of those who seem most rebellious against God, in word or deed, are at the place in their souls where they are not only ready, but eager, to repent and enter into a newness of life.

Therefore . . .

- Don't prejudge a person by his outer appearance—either of sin or of piety.
- Don't prejudge a person by his behavior—either for good or evil.
- Don't prejudge a person by his words—whether crude or refined.

The readiness level of a heart to know the Lord is known only to the Holy Spirit. And it is the Holy Spirit who will reveal the heart's readiness to you only as you enter into a life-changing conversation about Jesus Christ.

Let me elaborate this point a little further.

The secrets of a person's heart are known only to that person and to the Holy Spirit—including the secrets they have about God. The Scriptures say that it is the Lord who "searches all hearts and understands all the intent of the thoughts" (1 Chronicles 28:9). The apostle Paul wrote to the church at Corinth:

"Eye has not seen, nor ear heard,
Nor have entered into the heart of man
The things which God has prepared for those who love Him."

But God has revealed them to us through His Spirit. For the Spirit searches all things, yes, the deep things of God. For what man knows the things of a man except the spirit of the man which is in him? Even so no one knows the things of God except the Spirit of God. Now we have received, not the spirit of the world, but the Spirit who is from God, that we might know the things that have been freely given to us by God *(1 Corinthians 2:9–12).*

The inner spirit of another person can only be discerned spiritually. And, spiritual discernment is one of the gifts of the Holy Spirit (as described later by Paul in 1 Corinthians 12:10).

## Your Greatest Ally in Sharing Christ

The Word of God is your greatest tool. Your greatest ally as you share the Word is the Holy Spirit. In fact, you're His ally even more than He is yours.

His is the work of winning the lost—of preparing hearts, of transforming lives. You are invited to work alongside Him in a process in which He is already actively engaged!

The Holy Spirit desires that a person receive Christ Jesus far more than you do, and He will move within you and within the other person—as much as He is allowed to work—to bring the person to full birth, spiritually.

## The Holy Spirit "Gifts" You for the Process

It is the Holy Spirit who "gifts" you with power and other spiritual qualities you may need to engage in active soul winning.

Acts 1:8 tells us, "But ye shall receive power, after that the Holy Ghost is come upon you: and ye shall be witnesses unto me both in Jerusalem, and in all Judea, and in Samaria, and unto the uttermost part of the earth."

If you have received Jesus into your life and have received His Holy Spirit, then you are His witness. It's the very purpose His Holy Spirit dwells in you.

Some people have said to me through the years, "Well, Jerry, you're just gifted to be an active soul winner."

"Yes," I respond. "I have been gifted by the Holy Spirit to be His witness, just as every other Christian has been gifted by the Holy Spirit to be His witness."

## Spiritual Discernment Is Vitally Important

"Well," you may say, "I accept I'm gifted by the Holy Spirit, but I don't seem to be gifted with spiritual discernment."

When people say that to me, I generally respond, "How do you know?"

From my experience, the gift of discerning another person's spiritual condition is most evident once you have opened a conversation with someone about the Lord Jesus. Prior to such a conversation, I seldom have many clues from the Holy Spirit about what He is doing in a person's life. It simply isn't possible—or advisable—to try to "read" a person's spiritual state apart from your conversation with him about the Lord. You may be able to discern to some degree a person's "openness" as you approach him, but you can never fully discern his spiritual relationship with our heavenly Father.

In order to activate the gift of "discerning of spirits" in your life, you must first be willing to speak the name of Jesus, for it's at and to the name of Jesus that the spirit of a person responds.

If the person is not ready to accept the Lord, he will quickly respond toward that end when the name of Jesus is spoken. He may turn away, muttering some excuse to get away from you. At other times, he may attempt to change the topic of conversation very quickly—frequently to something as neutral as the weather, and sometimes to a topic that is more of a social issue than a matter of salvation. A few people react vehemently to the mention of his Name.

In all cases, I suggest to you that the response of the person to the name of Jesus will be such that you will be able to discern clearly the spiritual condition of that person.

At the opposite end of the spectrum are those who will respond to the name of Jesus with tears, or with a facial expression and other body language that gives you an impression they are clinging to your every word, or that they are searching for something of great value.

Again, I suggest to you that such an overt positive response to the name of Jesus will cause you to discern quite clearly that the spirit of this person is open to the Lord Jesus.

In between these extremes are those who respond in what appears to be a neutral or slightly favorable way. They may raise questions about Jesus, begin to talk about their church affiliation, or tell you about a spiritual event in their past.

In general, you can "discern" from their response that they are not closed to the Lord, and you can proceed with a conversation about Him. How you proceed is a question to ask the Holy Spirit!

## "Holy Spirit, What Shall I Say?"

Perhaps the most effective prayer you can ever pray as you converse with someone about the Lord Jesus is this,

*Holy Spirit, help me. Show me what You are doing in this person's life. Let me be sensitive to his need for You. Give me Your words to say!*

Ask for the Holy Spirit's enabling throughout your conversation with a person. Continually anticipate in your spirit: *What would Jesus Himself say or do in this situation to reconcile this person to our heavenly Father?* Or better, *How does He want to speak through me now?*

## Watch for the Holy Spirit to Give You a "Spiritual Prompting"

The Scriptures say, "That the righteous requirement of the law might be fulfilled in us who do not walk according to the flesh but according to the Spirit" (Romans 8:4). The "righteous requirement of the law" is the expression of the life of Jesus Christ in our lives. Jesus is the fulfillment of the Law. He is our righteousness. He lives in us. The full—or fulfilled—righteousness of the Lord Jesus happens through us, and it happens when we choose to walk after the Spirit.

What does that mean to us as active soul winners?

It means that the Holy Spirit has designed a way in which He desires for us to walk after Him as we share Christ with those who haven't received Him. The words I most often use in describing this are "spiritual prompting."

Have you ever watched a group of children giving a school play? Nearly always, there's a teacher offstage or in the orchestra pit who is available to feed one of the little actors lines, so easily forgotten in the bright stage lights and the excitement of standing before an audience.

We're in that same position, only more so. We, as little children following after the Spirit, don't have pre-rehearsed lines. *All* of our lines need to come from the Divine Prompter!

We feel virtually compelled to say the lines He gives to us.

The lines He gives us are frequently lines of Scripture which have been hidden away in our hearts.

The lines He gives us are ones that woo and extend God's genuine love to the person; they do not condemn. Very often this compassion far exceeds what we might normally feel.

The lines He gives us are sometimes surprising to us.

I was recently engaged in conversation with a man. We were already talking about spiritual matters when I suddenly felt compelled to ask this man a question that, within the context of our conversation thus far, seemed totally unrelated. I said, "The real root of the problem is [and I named the problem], isn't it?" He looked at me with a little surprise and then said genuinely, "Yes. That's really the problem." Recognizing the root of the problem allowed us to move very quickly to dealing with the problem. Within a few minutes, he was ready to receive the Lord into his life.

As the Holy Spirit leads us, we obey. We choose to follow and act on His promptings. We become sensitive to His direction, and we open our mouths and speak—boldly, with authority, and yet warmly and gently. Even as we speak, we are silently asking the Lord to give us His next words. We listen closely to how the person responds, and we listen closely to the Spirit to see what further truth He would have us share.

## The Holy Spirit's Guidance System

How does this prompting of the Holy Spirit manifest itself? Let me give you a very practical explanation.

Do you find yourself watching a person? Do you feel drawn to him in some way? Assume that it is the Holy Spirit who is leading you toward that person.

Do you have a feeling deep within that you understand a person you are watching from afar, just by reading her facial expressions? Assume that it is the Holy Spirit who is giving you that understanding.

Do you sense something beyond the surface level of a person's words—perhaps a feeling of pain, worry, or uneasiness? Assume that the Holy Spirit is the one who is giving you empathy with that person.

If your assumptions are incorrect and it isn't the Holy Spirit who is at work, you'll quickly discover that as you act on your assumption!

Move toward the person. Make eye contact. Smile and see if the smile is returned. If the person moves away, or rebuffs you, or turns his back to you, the Holy Spirit hasn't been the prompter! You can't know that, however, unless you make some kind of positive, gentle move toward the person.

Most of the time, I like to spend a few minutes getting to know a person and asking some questions so I get a feel for what he may or may not know about the Lord. Generally speaking, I'm looking for the "gaps" in the person's life. I'm looking for what he doesn't know about the Lord. Then, I seek to fill in those gaps.

Some people know very little. They may have heard about Jesus, but they may not know He died for their sins.

They may have known that Jesus was crucified on a cross and rose from the dead, but they may not know that He did it for their sins, so they might be forgiven.

They may know that Jesus died for the sins of the world, but they may not know how to relate to that fact, or how to receive Jesus into their lives as their personal Savior and Lord.

As I engage in conversation with a person, I'm continually looking for what more the Holy Spirit might add to this person's life. If the person is already a Christian, I'm looking for a way the Holy Spirit might bless or encourage this person in his spiritual growth. If the person doesn't know the Lord, I'm looking for an entry point to share more information about the Lord and what He has done for the person, how the Lord desires to give a person His forgiveness, peace, joy, and eternal life, and how to receive the Lord as Savior.

Did you ever study chemistry? Much of chemistry class involves identifying unknowns. The teacher gives a sample of a compound to a class and tells the students what kinds of tests to perform in order to evaluate the compound's properties and deduce its chemical makeup.

Engaging in a conversation about Christ is very much like chemistry class—you identify the spiritual unknowns about the person. Determine his relationship with the Lord, and then, under the guidance of the Holy Spirit, help move that person ever closer to a decision.

## Asking the Holy Spirit to Lead You Begins Long Before Your Encounter

The passage in Romans that tells us we are the fulfillment of the "righteous requirement of the law" goes on to say, "For as many as are led by the Spirit of God, these are sons of God" (Roman 8:14).

How can you know with assurance that you are being led and have been led?

It's only possible if you are willing to act on what you perceive to be His promptings in your spirit and check them out in your words and deeds toward others.

Let me put this in simple terms. You pray as you get up in the morning, "Lord, help me be an active soul winner. Lead me today. Guide my steps. Direct me to where You want me to go, and show me what You want me to do and say. As You lead me and show me, I'll do what You direct me to do."

All through the day, you are praying this prayer. And, all through the day, you are continually on the alert for possibilities.

About 4:00 P.M., your boss asks you to run an errand for him that's on the way to your house. He says, "Why don't you leave now to avoid the rush? No need to come back this afternoon. Go on home and bring me the item first thing in the morning." After you get the item for your boss, you stop at a quick-stop place to get a quart of milk. As you walk into the store, get the milk from the cooler, and prepare to pay for it, you realize that you are alone in the store with the cashier. You suddenly realize this has never happened before, even though you've been in this store more times than you can count.

Look at the cashier's face. Watch how he is moving. What do you see? You notice that he seems very tired, hunched over, a weary expression of his face. You sense that this man has not had a good day. You pray, "Holy Spirit, guide my words."

As you greet the cashier, you call him by the name on the tag he's wearing on his shirt, "Have you had an encouraging day, Bill?"

"Nope. Nothing has gone right today."

"Well, perhaps it's time things turned around. This may be the greatest day of your entire life!"

"What do you mean?"

"Well, Jesus Christ died for your sins so that you could be freed from all sin and guilt, have peace and joy in your life every day, and live in heaven with Him for all eternity. That's pretty encouraging news. It's made all the difference in my life. Would you like to receive Him into your life?"

"I dunno. What do I have to do?"

"Just ask Him to come into your life and be your Savior and Lord. You can do that very simply. Just say, 'Lord, I know I need you. Please have mercy on me, a sinner. Please forgive me of my sins and give me a new life on the inside. I need the joy and peace You alone can give me.' You'd like to experience that, wouldn't you, Bill?"

"Yeah, I would."

"Well, we can pray right now." You've noticed that there's still nobody in the store.

"I don't know how to pray."

"Oh, that's OK. I'll pray and you just repeat after me."

You lead Bill in a short prayer and then share with him, "Congratulations, Bill. You've just become a new creature in Christ Jesus." You go on to share in about three sentences that in order to grow as a new creation in Christ, Bill needs to get involved in a church where he'll hear the Word of God preached, to get a Bible and read it every day, and to talk to the Lord every day. "You can even do that here in the store, like now, when there's nobody around."

Bill is beaming. Without a doubt, you're the finest customer he's ever had come into the quick-stop store.

You're beaming, too! Another soul has been added to the Lord's kingdom.

Were you led by the Spirit?

Absolutely!

You continue on your way home, absolutely convinced anew that you *are* a son or a daughter of God!

## Approach or Avoid

When people are resisting God and hiding from the truth of God's Word, they'll literally run away from Him. The gospel requires a reaction from every person—either an openness and a moving toward it, or a hardness and a moving away from it.

One day I spotted a man on a subway train who was reading a Bible. "Pretty good Book you're reading," I said.

"Yes, it's the best," he replied. I asked him to read aloud a favorite Scripture and as he did, I noticed a young woman who had been sitting nearby jump up suddenly and move away quickly—just far enough away to be out of hearing distance.

Again, let's face a fact we've mentioned already.

## Most People Aren't Ready to Receive

Most people aren't ready to accept Jesus. Many are. But the majority are not.

It's vitally important that you face that fact and come to grips with it, or you will always feel a sense of disappointment, frustration, failure, and rejection. The majority of the people I have talked to through the years have *not* accepted Jesus Christ as their personal Savior. The fact is that most of the people with whom Jesus had contact during His ministry on this earth did not follow Him.

The Scriptures say that even after hearing Him speak and seeing His miracles, "many of His disciples went back and walked with Him no more" (John 6:66). Jesus Himself said,

"There are some of you who do not believe" and, "No one can come to Me unless it has been granted to him by My Father" and again, "No one can come to Me unless the Father who sent Me draws him" (John 6:64–65, 44).

Mathematically speaking, the Lord probably gets turned down three times out of four.

The important point, however, is to focus on the one person in four who does invite Him into his life.

Furthermore, you aren't really the one who does the preparing of a heart to know the Lord. *You are simply the one who does the harvesting—bringing the person to a point of decision.*

Let me remind you again of Jesus' words to His disciples: "The harvest truly is great, but the laborers are few; therefore pray the Lord of the harvest to send out laborers into His harvest" (Luke 10:2).

Note that Jesus calls His heavenly Father, the "Lord of the harvest." And again, He calls it "His harvest."

You're the gleaner. God is the grower.

It is the Lord who, through His Holy Spirit, speaks to a soul. It is the Lord who allows a seed of the gospel to take root deep within the soul of a human being, and there, to begin to grow to the point of harvest. It is the Lord who brings a person to new birth in "the fullness of time"—not only in the life of that person, but in the life of the world, so that a person might be born anew healthy, and rightly fitted for a divine purpose. Yes, it is the Lord who is the grower of souls.

Many of us take on the responsibility of trying to "grow" people. We become frustrated when they don't grow fast enough, or in the ways in which we wish they would. We usually like to hurry the process. But growing souls isn't our job.

Our job is to:

- plant seeds of the gospel,
- water those seeds with encouraging and convicting words given to us by the Holy Spirit, and
- give people an opportunity to be "harvested"—to make a decision to open their lives to Jesus Christ.

## The Seed Tests the Soil

Your job as an active soul winner is to test the soil. You know that the seed is good if it's a seed of the gospel. I like the way the Amplified Bible describes the Word of God:

> For the Word that God speaks is alive and full of power—making it active, operative, energizing, and effective . . . exposing and sifting and analyzing and judging the very thoughts and purposes of the heart *(Hebrews 4:12 AMPLIFIED BIBLE)*.

Those same descriptive words apply to a living seed. A seed presents a challenge to the soil. And if the soil is ready—if it is moist enough, fertile enough, and exposed to enough warmth from the sun—the soil will allow that seed to germinate, take root, and grow. If the soil is too hard, too rocky, too cold, or too dry, the seed will lie dormant.

Your job as an active soul winner is not to prepare the soil, but to sow the good seed.

This was the message of the parable that Jesus taught about a sower who went out and sowed seeds. Some fell on hard ground, some grew up in thorny ground, some couldn't sprout because of the rocks in the soil. But that which fell on good soil sprang up and bore fruit—thirtyfold, sixtyfold, even a hundredfold. (See Matthew 13:3–9, 18–23.)

You can't always tell what kind of soil lies under people's crusty outer-countenance. You can't tell how dry or stony their inner heart may be. You can't tell how much the Son has already warmed their hearts. That, however, isn't really your job. Your job is to sow seed.

The seed—the Word of God, the name of Jesus, the telling of the gospel—will test the soil.

The apostle Paul said, "I planted, Apollos watered, but God gave the increase. So then neither he who plants is anything, nor he who waters, but God who gives the increase" (1 Corinthians 3:6–7).

## Pass It On—Freely

In Matthew 10:8, Jesus said: "Freely you have received, freely give."

What have you received?

The abundance of grace. The gift of righteousness. These are the things that have been given to you as free gifts. You received them by faith from Jesus Christ who gave them to you. Now it is your joy to give them by faith to others.

The Holy Spirit will help you do it!

# AVOIDING PITFALLS AND SLAYING DRAGONS

I recently asked the man sitting next to me on an airplane several questions. He answered each one, "No," "No," "Yes," "No," "No." He did tell me he was a physician.

I asked him, "Are you aware of any spiritual awakening in your patients?" He said, "No."

I asked him if people seemed to be experiencing more fear and stress in their lives. He said, "No, not in the people I see or work with."

I found it incredible that this man, a medical doctor, wasn't more aware of God at work or of people in need. I concluded that he was very likely spiritually blinded. (Spiritual blindness has nothing to do with one's intellectual, economic, or physical condition.)

I knew there was no need to carry my conversation with this man any further. I had hit a brick wall in my ability to share the Lord with him that day.

When I receive a response that's very closed and curt, I don't press the point of sharing the gospel. Jesus Himself said, "Do not give what is holy unto the dogs; nor cast your pearls before swine, lest they trample them under their feet, and turn and tear you in pieces" (Matthew 7:6).

It's the work of the Holy Spirit to tear down a brick wall of resistance. However, there are two things I do:

• Attempt to share as much of the gospel as possible.

I might say, "Well, the most encouraging news I've heard lately is how many people are coming to know the Lord as their personal Savior. They're experiencing the forgiveness of their sins, a freedom from guilt, and a joy and peace they've never known before. You'll probably find yourself thinking more about that in the next few days."

- Intercede silently that the Holy Spirit will work in the person's life.

In this particular case, I knew I could silently intercede for this man, praying that the Lord would bind the spirits that were blinding him to the truth and open his ears, heart, and mind to the gospel.

# Don't Add Further Injury to the Spiritually Blind or Deaf

The apostle Paul wrote, "All things are of God, who has reconciled us to Himself through Jesus Christ, and has given us the ministry of reconciliation, that is, that God was in Christ reconciling the world to Himself, not imputing their trespasses to them, and has committed to us the word of reconciliation" (2 Corinthians 5:18–19).

Sharing the Lord Jesus with others is a ministry of reconciliation. Salvation brings a person to a point where he is truly reconciled to the Father.

Satan leads all people to believe that something is wrong with them that God can't fix. The fact is that we are the victims of Satan's abuse. We've been under false ownership and bad management.

The good news is that the Lord Jesus Christ came to fix us, regardless of how badly we may be broken, bruised, or battered. Jesus came to reopen us to the world under new management—His management of the Holy Spirit. He gives us His Spirit not only to correct the previous abuse in our lives and cover it with His love, but to make us new creations in His image and likeness so that we can live and operate as Jesus did when He was on this earth.

Jesus said He came to bind up the broken hearted, to bring recovery and to preach good news to the poor of spirit. Our mission is His mission!

The words we speak to another person must be ones that build up, lead forward, and promote reconciliation.

Salvation involves so much more than avoiding hell or eternal damnation.

## It's More Than Just Avoiding Hell

As you share with people who grew up in church, but who never received Jesus Christ as their personal Savior and Lord, you may find they connect "salvation" with "escaping hell." They understand salvation in these terms: "A person is saved so he won't go to hell" or, "If you aren't saved, you're going to hell."

As true as the linkage between salvation and eternal damnation may be, I seldom use that approach with people. Instead, I hold out what Jesus promises to those who receive Him and confess Him in their lives. Jesus promises:

- Your sins will be forgiven—no matter how bad, how many, how old, or how new the sins might be. Another way to say this is . . .
- You will be free of the burden of guilt.
- You can receive the Holy Spirit into your life. The Spirit of Truth, the great Comforter, the one who is called alongside us as our Divine Helper is made available to every believer.
- You will experience the peace and joy of the Lord.
- You will have the assurance of everlasting life and of an eternal home with the Lord in heaven.
- You can be made a new creature and have a new beginning in life—"Therefore, if anyone is in Christ, he is a new creation; old things have passed away; behold, all things have become new" (2 Corinthians 5:17).

The good things that the Lord promises us through receiving Him as Savior are so wonderful and so compelling, they attract and win the heart. Rather than ask—or demand—that people run from hell, why not invite them to run toward the outstretched arms of Jesus and toward a heavenly home?

## Emphasize God's Love

The love of God is irresistible. A person may try to resist it but, ultimately, it is hard to refuse the greatest love a person can ever know.

At some point in my conversation with a person, I try to share God's love with him in one or more of these ways:

- "God loves you."
- "God loves you so much that He sent His Son, Jesus Christ, to die on a cross for you so that you can be set free from your sins and live with the Lord forever."
- "God loves you right where you are, right now."
- "God loves you so much that He sent me to share that news with you."

Most people are desperate to hear that God loves them, even if they won't admit it to you. The news of God's love is like balm on an open wound. Pour it out generously!

## Hard Sell or Soft Sell?

Some people prefer a straightforward approach. They like simple, direct questions. They respond simply and directly.

Others need time to engage in a relationship—to exchange pleasant comments, to explore ideas and ask questions, to share.

Be sensitive to both types of people, and adjust your method to them. Don't expect them to change their personalities in order to receive your message. I always . . .

- choose *not* to make demands, either in my tone of voice or in the words I use.
- choose *not* to raise my voice.
- choose *not* to trap a person—neither to corner them physically nor in a conversation.
- choose *not* to lay any more burden of guilt upon them than they are already feeling.

I *do* choose to maintain eye contact, bring the conversation to a close with a positive word about Jesus or a prayer (even if the person chooses not to receive Him into his life), and I *do* state as much of the gospel message and the Word of God as I can in the time available.

## Avoid Arguments

What do you do if the person says he doesn't believe the Bible?

I don't spend a lot of time on apologetics—arguing the truth of God's Word. God's Word is true, and we can only experience that fact as the Holy Spirit imprints it on our hearts and as we see that the truth of the Bible works as we live out its commands.

Jesus asked His disciples, "Who do men say that I, the Son of Man, am?" and then followed up their answer by asking, "Who do you say that I am?" Peter responded, "You are the Christ, the Son of the living God." And Jesus said, "Blessed are you, Simon Bar-Jonah, for flesh and blood has not revealed this to you, but My Father who is in heaven." (See Matthew 16:13, 15–17.) The truth about Jesus is a revelation from the Father. This is true about everything Jesus said and did in the Bible and for every aspect of the Old Testament which points to Jesus and which Jesus fulfilled.

You cannot convince someone else that God's Word is true. Your heavenly Father must do that.

You can teach people what you know of God's Word, if they are interested in hearing it.

You can pray for them.

And you can simply say to those who protest against the Bible in their hearts and claim they don't believe it, "I believe the Bible *is* true. I base my belief on what it's meant in my life and on how I've seen it work in the lives of others I know who believe and obey its teaching."

In other words, you can give a personal witness to the truth of the Bible without entering into debates on certain verses or passages.

I avoid arguments as much as possible because . . .

- I've found that most arguments are simply a diversion. The person is trying to avoid the real truth about Jesus Christ by calling into question a passage of Scripture. Recognize the diversion for what it is—an attempt to sidestep the truth. Bring the conversation back to Jesus Christ and the centrality of the Cross. Keep it focused there.
- I've found that most arguments aren't resolved. The person who argues about a verse of Scripture is not going to be convinced by you. He has usually adopted a deeply entrenched position about that verse of Scripture, and he isn't going to let go of it easily. Trust the Holy Spirit to continue to work in his life and to soften his position so that someday he might come to know the Lord.

Even if you win an argument, you'll likely lose the opportunity to win that person to Christ.

I'm speaking, of course, about arguments based on doctrinal issues. You certainly can respond to a person's negative statements.

# Reasoning and Persuading Are Not Arguing

The Scriptures say, "'Come now, and let us reason together,' says the LORD" (Isaiah 1:18). Reasoning together is not arguing. An argument is a combative conversation in which sides are taken, positions are drawn and evidence is put forth to pull a person across an imaginary line in the philosophical sands.

Reasoning together is an entirely scriptural activity to undertake. It is usually an activity for believers—searching the Scriptures for assurance, edification, and strength.

In Acts 28:23, Paul received people into his lodging on an appointed day and "he explained and solemnly testified of the kingdom of God, persuading them concerning Jesus from both the Law of Moses and the Prophets, from morning till evening." Persuasion is an act of wooing those who are neutral to confess Jesus Christ as Lord. We *are* called to persuade.

The apostle Paul openly declared to the Corinthians, "We persuade men" (2 Corinthians 5:11).

Persuasion, however, is not argument either. To be persuaded, a person must have opened his mind to some degree toward the gospel, and he must have put himself into a position of being willing to hear. Even King Agrippa had that stance as he heard Paul's defense. He said, "You almost persuade me to become a Christian" (Acts 26:28). Agrippa's encounter with Paul was not one marked by argument. It was one in which he heard Paul out.

I do not find a place in the Scriptures where argument is encouraged or where argumentation results in lost souls being won. Argumentation is combative. It polarizes. It further entrenches the lost person into a position that he becomes determined to defend.

I would rather walk away from argument and leave the person with a positive, authoritative word from the Lord spoken in peace, than to engage in a verbal or doctrinal fistfight that results in all parties being bruised. There are too many people ready to respond to the Lord to spend time in what may further alienate a person from Him.

To avoid arguments, of course, is also to avoid those issues which are so often divisive in an active soul winning situation. I rarely discuss controversial political issues with people. I turn conversations away from matters of doctrine. I try to avoid giving an opinion about anything that doesn't relate directly to the Lord Jesus and how He can meet that person's need.

## Avoid Questions that Have No Answer

You will never be able to explain certain issues to the satisfaction of another person. The answer simply doesn't lie on this side of eternity. Suffering is one of those issues. Rejection by loved ones is another. You can spend hours trying to find an answer or an idea that satisfies the person, but generally those hours are spent without reaching a definitive conclusion or reaching an answer that is watertight.

Rather than attempt to explain what I do not understand

about God, I attempt to turn a conversation toward what I do understand. I do understand that . . .

- God loves. (See John 3:16).
- God cares. (See 1 Peter 5:7.)
- God heals and makes whole. (The entire ministry of Jesus provides this evidence. See also James 5:15–16.)
- God forgives and cleanses us from sin and guilt. (See 1 John 1:7.)
- God restores and raises anew. (See 2 Corinthians 1:9–10).
- God gives eternal life. (See 1 John 5:11.)

The Cross embodies all of those acts of God. Stay focused on the Cross. Stay focused on what you do know about the Lord—that He desires above all that men and women should come to know Him, receive Him, trust in Him, and abide in Him even as He abides in them.

# Getting a Person to Open Up—Gently!

Our tendency seems to be to ask people who we perceive are hurting, "Is something wrong?"

The hurting person will very often answer "no" or shrug off the question, even if something is really troubling her deeply. I've found a more effective question is: "Something is wrong, isn't it?" For some reason, stating that you perceive something to be wrong puts you on the person's side and shows that you have empathy with him. The person nearly always responds, "Yes."

A second tendency we have in following up is to say, "What can I do?" The person in need may not know what you can do to help. He may know and be ashamed, afraid, or unsure about asking you to help. I've found a better response to be any one of these questions:

- "You've been hurt by someone, haven't you?"
- "Something has gone wrong, hasn't it?"
- "Something negative is coming at you, isn't it?"
- "Something is causing you pain, isn't it?"

You may say, "That sorta sounds like guessing."

I used to think that it was, too. I'd find myself asking a question and thinking as I asked it, "Why are you asking that, Wiles? You're stabbing in the dark." Still, the more I asked questions such as these, the more I found that I was getting "yes" answers and that people were responding to the questions genuinely—opening up to tell me more specifically what it was that was causing their misery. I finally decided that the Holy Spirit can guide our guessing and our questions just as much as He can guide our statements and actions.

Even if you are wrong in your line of questioning, the person is likely to respond, "No, that's not it" and tell you about the real root of the problem

## Getting to the Root

Why ask such questions at all? Because it's important that you get to the root of a person's spiritual situation as quickly as possible. The root is where the Holy Spirit seeks to lay the axe of redemption and bring about newness and restoration.

It's extremely important to . . .

## Ask the Right Questions to Get the Right Answer

I rarely ask a person, "Are you a Christian?"

Many people equate Christianity with church attendance. Some people assume that if they attend, or have ever attended, a Protestant or Catholic church, they are Christians. Many, many people assume that if they were baptized as a child, they are Christians.

Others think of themselves as being Christians because they aren't anything else! Some people come to the conclusion that they are Christians through a process of elimination—"Well, I'm not a Hindu, I'm not a Buddhist, I'm not a Jew, I'm not an atheist, so I must be a Christian." Still others have heard that the United States is a "Christian nation," so they assume that because they are citizens of the United States, they are Christians.

Neither church membership, nor infant baptism, nor a personal philosophy, nor general citizenship is the same as having a personal relationship with the Lord Jesus Christ as Savior, being filled with His Holy Spirit, and having an assurance that your sins have been forgiven and that your eternal home will be with the Lord.

I also avoid asking, "Are you born-again?" without some explanation.

So many people have so many definitions for that phrase, they may say "yes" for the wrong reasons, or they may say "no" even though they have received Jesus Christ into their lives!

Instead of asking people an "Are you a _____?" type of question, I prefer to present the gospel message first and then ask them to respond to it.

If I must use a question in leading a person to the point of decision, I do not say, "Would you like to become a Christian?" Instead, I ask, "Would you like to receive the Lord Jesus Christ into your life as your personal Savior?"

For example, I once struck up a conversation with a young man who was setting up a morning prayer breakfast at which I was scheduled to speak. I had arrived early for a time of prayer and preparation in the banquet hall, and he was supervising the staff as they set up the tables in preparation of the guests.

After a few casual comments with this young man, I said, "I'm scheduled to be on the program today. Would you mind if I rehearsed with you a little of what I'm planning to say?"

He said, "Sure, go ahead."

I said, "I'm going to be sharing today about the Lord Jesus Christ and what it means to me that He died on the cross for my sins." I went on to give him a paragraph or two of summary about who Jesus is and how to receive the Lord.

I then asked him, "Have you ever received the Lord?"

He said he hadn't. I said, "You'd like to be forgiven of your sins and know you had everlasting life, though, wouldn't you?

He said he would. We prayed together and as we finished, the people began to arrive for the prayer breakfast, so we went our separate ways.

During my presentation, I started to share with the group gathered what had happened. I said, "Let me tell you what happened earlier this morning to my friend Walter." Just at that moment, Walter entered the banquet room, and he assumed that I had just introduced him. He came forward and gave his own testimony to the people about what had happened to him! Praise God for those who experience a new birth in the Lord and who haven't yet been told they should be scared to share the news with anyone else!

## "I Think I've Been Born Again"

Occasionally you'll encounter somebody who will respond to you with a statement such as this: "I think I've done this" or, "Well, I was baptized as a child, is that what you mean?"

The person who is truly born again of the spirit knows he is. That is not to say a Christian will never have doubts about his salvation.

The person who questions whether he has been born again usually falls into one of two categories. Either he was baptized as a child or had an experience as a child that he thinks was a time of being spiritually born. Or, he needs assurance that the confession of faith he has made really did the job.

I usually try to help the person evaluate the experience they had.

People will often readily admit that the experience they had in the past didn't make a difference in their hearts and wills.

When in doubt about what to do in evaluating or discussing a person's past spiritual experiences, I suggest this principle: take them where they're at today. If the person has been genuinely born anew in the spirit, he won't mind praying with you and sealing that fact. If the person has not had a genuine encounter with the Lord, your prayer with him can resolve the issue for him.

I also do not ask, "Do you know the Lord?"

When I asked this question people tended to respond, "Sure. I grew up in a Christian family. I went to church as a child."

If this line of questioning arises, I ask, "Well, is there any time in your life when you came to see yourself as a sinner in need of the Lord, when you asked the Lord to come into your life as your Savior and to free you from the burden of sin and guilt?"

The answer is usually, "No."

"Well," I say, "you have probably wondered down through the years if the Lord had something more for you, or wondered how you might know Him better, haven't you?"

Most people who get this far in a conversation will nod or say, "Yes."

I then share with them how they can receive the Lord right then and there.

I once met a waitress who told me that she knew the Lord. I asked her how she had come to know Him and she responded, "I went to a missions school when I was growing up in Bolivia."

I shared with her a little more about what it means to have a personal relationship with Jesus Christ as Savior and Lord. She seemed interested, but we didn't have an opportunity to share further since the restaurant was very busy. I lingered over my meal until the restaurant had nearly cleared after the noon rush hour.

As I went to the cash register to pay for my meal, I began to share about the Lord with the cashier. He was ready to accept the Lord, and within a minute or two after I started sharing with him, I said, "Carlos, you're ready to receive the Lord into your life right now, aren't you?" He said, "Yes," and we began to pray. As we prayed, I realized that this waitress was standing right next to us, and she was repeating the words with us!

## Examining Ourselves

The apostle Paul wrote to the Corinthians, "Examine yourselves as to whether you are in the faith. Test yourselves. Do you not know yourselves, that Jesus Christ is in you?—unless indeed you are disqualified" (2 Corinthians 13:5).

Let's recognize that some people have had a counterfeit conversion experience. They may have been convinced in their minds, stirred in their emotions, walked down an aisle, and made some decision. And yet, they walked away from that experience to continue to live a "disqualified" life. The experience brought about no changes in them—of heart, word, or deed.

Other people have had what I call a psychological conversion. They have made up their minds about Jesus, but their spirits have not been regenerated. They have accepted the historical Jesus, but they have never encountered the living Christ.

As you share the truth with a person, he will generally come to a statement about what his experience has been. He'll not only express it to you but, in so doing, he'll see his past action more clearly for what it was.

I once had a man say to me, "I've been baptized."

I asked him, "Yes, but you know that there's more to life than what you've discovered, and you are longing for a more intimate relationship with the Lord, aren't you?"

"Yes," he said.

People who say, "I've been baptized" are usually hoping that the experience they had is enough and yet, at the same time, most of them are living with doubt and uncertainty.

I used to spend a great deal of time trying to analyze whether a person's past experience with the Lord was sufficient, correct, valid. I don't do that as much anymore.

The person who has had a genuine conversion of their spirit knows it. They will look you right in the eye and say, "Yes, I've experienced a spiritual birth. I know Jesus as my Savior and Lord."

A person who wonders about a past action—be it baptism, joining a church, going through a confirmation or catechism class, raising a hand at an altar call, responding to a Sunday school teacher's prayer, or whatever the action may have been—is someone with whom you can always say, "Well, you can be sure that you know the Lord Jesus Christ as your personal Savior and Lord today. Right now! You can seal this once and for all in your life and never have to wonder about it again or question whether a past experience was the right one."

No matter what past experiences a person may have had—even perfect church attendance or denominational membership for thirty years—I attempt to bring that person to an experience in which they acknowledge the Lord in prayer.

Sometimes after prayer, they will say, "Yes, I have an assurance now that what once happened to me was a genuine spiritual rebirth." Usually what has happened is that the person, through prayer, has been released of a great deal of doubt that has held him in bondage through the years. All Christians should come to a settled assurance and confidence that they belong to the Lord and are kept by His power.

Such a prayer has incredible value in a person's life. It seals for him the redemptive work that the Holy Spirit has done.

For others, a prayer of renewed commitment gives them an adult reference point to which they can always look back and say, "I remember that day."

For still others, a prayer of renewed commitment releases the power of the Holy Spirit in their lives. They may have repented of their sins and been baptized—as Peter preached—but failed to receive the fullness and power of the Holy Spirit working in their lives.

Share with the person the confidence you have that his confession of faith is now sufficient. Show him Romans 10:13 in your New Testament, and let him read it aloud for himself, "Whosoever calls on the name of the LORD shall be saved." If you don't have a New Testament with you, write down the verse and encourage him to look it up and read it aloud for himself in the privacy of his own home. By the way, ninety percent of all Americans, according to recent surveys, have at least one copy of the Bible in their homes.

Don't leave a person wondering if a past experience qualifies them for eternal life. Leave them with a present-day experience that assures them of the fact!

# The Tattoo Said "Sinner"

I was in a park recently, and I spotted a scruffy young man with tattoos on his arms sitting on a bench. My teenaged son and I sat down at the other end of the bench. I mentioned to the young man that my son and I found his tattoos interesting, and he held out his arms so we could examine them a little more closely. I noticed that the one up by his shoulder clearly said "Sinner."

I mentioned it to the man and said, "Boy, that's an interesting one." He nodded and I went on, "You really see yourself that way, don't you?"

He said, "Yeah, I do."

I shared with him a little about the grace and love of God. He was a person who felt that he had sinned too much in his life to ever be forgiven by God.

I've noticed that sinners who have heard about Jesus and what He did on the cross tend to fall into two broad categories. They either think they are too bad to be saved, or they feel they are good enough and don't need to be saved. This man was in the former category.

In each case, it helps to simply redefine what it is that makes a person a sinner and to restate what Jesus said He would do.

Both categories of people are under some degree of conviction, at some level. Those who feel they are too bad to be forgiven tend to be weighed down with guilt and feelings of condemnation.

Those who feel they are too good to need to be forgiven are very often victims of their own striving. They are frequently frustrated and uptight, forever justifying their position, criticizing anyone who might try to label them as a sinner, trying to walk the straight and narrow and avoid slipping into a sin that would mar their unsullied record.

A true believer in the Lord Jesus knows two things about himself. First, he's a sinner. The redeemed person readily admits that he, in the flesh, is subject to the flesh, and that without the redeeming spirit and love of Christ shed abroad in his heart, he is a sinner. Second, the true believer knows that he has been forgiven by the Lord Jesus and that he is free of the burden and guilt of sin, not through anything that he has done, but through what Jesus Christ did on the cross.

As you talk with people, watch for them to take one of these two positions.

## What to Say to the Too-Bad-to-Be-Saved Person

If a person tells me he is too bad to be saved or that he has committed too many sins, I usually say, "You may say that. Other people may have told you that. But that's not what God says." I usually share one or more of these verses with the person:

> If we confess our sins, He is faithful and just to forgive us our sins and to cleanse us from all unrighteousness (1 John 1:19).

> God demonstrated His own love toward us, in that while we were still sinners, Christ died for us (Romans 5:8).

> For I am persuaded that neither death nor life, nor angels nor principalities nor powers, nor things present nor things to come, nor height nor depth, nor any other created thing, shall be able to separate us from the love of God which is in Christ Jesus our Lord (Romans 8:38–39).

## What to Say to the Too-Good-to-Need-Salvation Person

To those who think they are beyond the need for salvation, I remind them of Romans 3:23—"For all have sinned and fall short of the glory of God." I then say, "The good news is that even though we fall short of God's glory, we can experience forgiveness and know with assurance that we have an eternal home in heaven. We can put ourselves into a position to receive even more of God's blessings and power into our lives."

Occasionally, I'll have the person read Romans 3:9–19 aloud with me, which says:

> What then? Are we better than they? Not at all. For we have previously charged both Jews and Greeks that they are all under sin.
>   As it is written:

> "There is none righteous, no, not one;
> There is none who understands;
> There is none who seeks after God.
> They have all turned aside;
> They have together become unprofitable;
> There is none who does good, no, not one."
> "Their throat is an open tomb;
> With their tongues they have practiced deceit";
> "The poison of asps is under their lips";
> "Whose mouth is full of cursing and bitterness."
> "Their feet are swift to shed blood;
> Destruction and misery are in their ways;
> And the way of peace they have not known."
> "There is no fear of God before their eyes."

Now we know that whatever the law says, it says to those who are under the law, that every mouth may be stopped, and all the world may become guilty before God.

It's very difficult to read that passage and not conclude that *all* are sinners without the Lord.

A friend of mine uses this question in confronting those who feel they are good enough and don't need salvation, "Wouldn't you like to know for sure that your ultimate home will be in heaven?"

## The Sincere Questioner

Occasionally you'll meet sincere questioners. They'll usually phrase their doubt or concern in statements such as, "I've always wondered about that part in the Bible where . . ." or, "What do you think about that part in the Bible where . . . ."

Share what you can with these people. And, at the same time, recognize that soul winning and Bible teaching are two distinct ministries. As you share, make Jesus and what He did on the cross central to your explanation. Show how the passage in question relates to the shed blood of Jesus and His death and resurrection.

Some people do have a concern about whether they have blasphemed the Holy Spirit. It's pretty amazing to me that of all the statements that Jesus made, the one in which He speaks of the unpardonable sin of blasphemy against the

Holy Spirit seems to be the one most people remember if they are in the category of "I'm too bad to be forgiven." The point is, these people want desperately to be forgiven, and they are deeply afraid that they may have crossed the line.

You can always assure people that if they are concerned about the question, they haven't committed the unpardonable sin. The Holy Spirit is still working in their lives. In fact, He has brought them to this very point where their question can be answered, the issue can be settled, and today is the day they can know the reality of Jesus Christ in their lives. You can readily say, "I'm here as living proof to you that God still cares about you. He's still reaching out to you. And He's offering you this chance to repent of your sins, to accept Jesus Christ and what He did on the cross for you, to be forgiven of all your sins, and to enter into a peace and joy He has prepared just for you! If that wasn't true, the Holy Spirit would never have led me to talk to you."

Most people don't want to argue about the Scriptures. In fact, when you talk to people about the Lord, the vast majority of them will never even bring up the Bible or what they think of it.

## The Test for the Spirits

On occasion—I don't find this to be the norm—a person may speak to you in a way that will lead you to question whether the person is speaking their own opinion, or whether they are speaking under the bondage or influence of an evil spirit. At other times, you may hear something from a person that may seem a little "off" to you, but you may not be able to clearly discern whether the person is agreeing with you as a believer, or whether he is caught in the web of deceit that snares those who are the victims of cults.

The Scriptures provide us a clear criterion for determining whether a spirit is of God or not.

Beloved, do not believe every spirit, but test the spirits, whether they are of God; because many false prophets have gone out into the world. By this you know the Spirit of God: Every spirit that confesses that Jesus Christ has come in the flesh is of God, and every spirit that does not confess that Jesus Christ has come in the flesh is not of God *(1 John 4:1–3)*.

You can ask a person, "Is Jesus Christ the Son of God who appeared in the flesh on this earth?" If the answer is no—and usually you can conclude that the answer is no if it's anything other than a clear yes—then you are dealing with someone who is not a believer in the Lord Jesus.

# Taking Dominion over Evil Spirits

Jesus Christ conquered sin, death, and hell on the cross, and He destroyed Satan's power and control over our lives.

Most people don't realize that they are operating under one of two influences: the influence of the Holy Spirit or the influence of unholy spirits. Most people think they're "doing their own thing" when they aren't following God. The truth is that they are doing Satan's bidding and don't know it. They are slaves to a master they haven't yet acknowledged.

A person is under the dominion of either the devil or the Lord. The Bible only speaks of two kingdoms: one of light ruled by the Lord Jesus Christ, the other of darkness ruled by the fallen Lucifer and his demonic minions.

Satan specializes in misusing, abusing, and prostituting our humanity. He does a better job on some people than on others. But all of us are victims to some extent of "child abuse." As a child of God, we've all been victims of the devil's abuse at some point in our lives.

Jesus destroyed the devil's authority over mankind. When we align ourselves with the Lord Jesus—through an act of our will in choosing to repent of our sins, inviting Jesus into our lives, and making a choice to follow Him and be filled with and guided by His Spirit—the devil no longer has a right to us. The devil may try to exert his influence over us, but it's now our privilege in Christ to resist him, saying to him, "Be gone," and watch him flee. The Bible clearly promises, "Resist the devil and he will flee from you" (James 4:7).

Our role after our spiritual birth is to be people who reign, who triumph, who win, who are victorious over the wiles of the devil. New Testament words that describe the believer are "overcoming" words.

We no longer need to be dominated by our circumstances, by the world, the flesh, and the devil. That doesn't mean that we will be forever in a state of happiness, wealth, and health. It does mean that no matter in what situation we find ourselves, we can have an inner stability that endures. Our faith can remain steadfast, as 1 Peter 5:8-9 so vividly describes: "Your adversary the devil walks about like a roaring lion, seeking whom he may devour. Resist him, steadfast in the faith."

Furthermore, we—through the power of the Holy Spirit— have authority over evil spirits. The only thing that the devil has left is a lie—a "roar." Notice that Peter said the devil comes "like a roaring lion." He isn't a lion. Only Jesus is the reigning Lion of Judah. But, he can come roaring as a lion— with a lying roar—pretending to be a real lion with real power when actually that power was stripped from him by the Lord Jesus the moment when we repented of our sins and acknowledged Jesus as our Lord, Savior, and the Christ.

## You Have Been Given the Power to Back Up the Command

The Scriptures say, "Be not deceived." Don't give in to fear at the devil's roar! Don't be tricked by just a roar.

Jesus promised, "All authority has been given to Me in heaven and on earth. Go therefore and make disciples of all the nations, baptizing them in the name of the Father and of the Son and of the Holy Spirit, teaching them to observe all things that I have commanded you; and lo, I am with you always, even to the end of the age" (Matthew 28:18-20).

Again God's Word says, "He [the Holy Spirit] who is in you is greater than he [the enemy of your souls] who is in the world" (1 John 4:4).

Jesus doesn't ask you to do something He doesn't equip you with power to do. Read Acts 1:8 again: "You shall receive power when the Holy Spirit has come upon you; and you shall be witnesses to Me."

How do you receive that power? Peter said at the conclusion of his great sermon on the day of Pentecost, "Repent and let every one of you be baptized in the name of Jesus Christ for the remission of sins; and you shall receive the gift of the Holy Spirit" (Acts 2:38). You *shall* receive.

You receive by faith in the same way that you receive Christ Jesus as your Savior, by faith.

How do you take dominion over the enemy of your souls when he comes roaring at us? By faith.

Resist the devil's roar. Stand firm in your resolve that Jesus *is* Lord, *will forever be* Lord, and *is now* Lord in the situation confronting you. And tell the devil he must go, in the name of Jesus.

The authority that was given to Jesus has been given to us to use.

From time to time you will encounter those who are held in bondage by the devil's roar. Generally speaking, these are people who exhibit a great deal of fear. It's as if they are paralyzed by the devil's lie. Take action to release them from that paralysis.

# A Prayer for Release from Fear's Bondage

From time to time you'll engage in a conversation with a person who will seem interested in what you are saying but who will exhibit a fear of receiving the Lord. He might say such things as, "I'd like to accept the Lord, but . . ." or, "I want to do this, but . . ." or "This makes sense to me, but I just don't know . . . ."

Take authority over that excuse. Ask the person immediately, "Why don't you let me pray about that—that you'll have the freedom to make this decision to receive the Lord Jesus?" And then pray,

*Heavenly Father, I ask You to free [the person's name], in the name of Jesus, from any tormenting thoughts or plaguing doubts that are keeping [the person's name] from making a decision to receive Your Son, the Lord Jesus Christ, into his heart as his personal Savior and Lord.*

Some people are held in the bondage of the enemy. It may be by a decades-old hurt from childhood, a plaguing memory, a deep-seated doubt, or an undefinable fear.

Their spirits are willing to receive the Lord, but the enemy is holding something over their heads that is binding them and keeping them from moving forward. Recognize this situation for the spiritual battle that it is. Take authority. Ask the Holy Spirit to do the releasing in their spirits. Use the name of Jesus with confidence.

After you've prayed with a person, ask again, "Do you feel you can now receive the Lord Jesus into your life?" In my experience, I've found that in many cases the person says yes.

People who say "I'd like to" or "I want to" are just one step away from saying "I will." Help them to take that final step!

# ▲ TEN

# CLOSING THE ENCOUNTER

Every salesman knows that the most important part of any deal is "the close." The sales representative can get an appointment with a prospective buyer, give his presentation, and answer all the questions asked about the product. Yet, if he never asks the customer to buy, the presentation has no point. The appointment bears no fruit.

After I've shared the gospel with a person, I find it most effective to ask the person, "Would you like to receive Christ into your life right now?" Or, I might say, "Let me lead us in prayer, and you can respond to the Lord right now."

## Give the Person an Opportunity

It's not your responsibility to get a person to respond positively to the sharing of the gospel or to the name of Jesus. It's only your responsibility to give him an opportunity to respond positively.

If you don't give people an opportunity, they most likely won't respond. If you do give them an opportunity, it's up to them how they will respond. Their response is directly related to what the Holy Spirit is doing in their lives.

However, to fail to give a person an opportunity to respond to the gospel puts the responsibility on you.

That's a sobering reality.

## Different Facets but the Same Basics

The basics of being "born anew" spiritually, or of receiving Christ, are the same for each person. That's true in natural birth, too. Women and their physicians have noted it time and time again, "Each pregnancy is different." The point is, each baby is different. And yet each baby is born in pretty much the same way. Intense contractions result in a baby being pushed through the birth canal and into a new world, followed by separation from the mother as the umbilical cord is cut. A gasp or cry comes from the baby as it begins to breathe on its own, and an eager desire for nourishment soon follows. There are slight variations on that theme, of course, but the natural flow of birthing events is consistent, even though individual differences may keep doctors on their toes or put nurses into near-frantic motion.

The birthing analogy is one Jesus Himself used in describing what happens to a person when he is spiritually reborn by the Holy Spirit. The person is unique. The incidents leading up to a person's spiritual birth are unique. The process of birthing is similar to that experienced by all other persons who have received Christ.

Birthing in our world today can come either by natural means, or through a cesarean section. Birthing spiritually also happens by generally two methods: petitioning or confessing.

## Petitioning and Confessing

In petitioning, which we usually think of as prayer, the person is *asking* the Lord to do a work in his or her life. In confessing, the person is *acknowledging* the work that the Lord is doing. Both methods arrive at the same point: accepting what the Lord has done and receiving Him into one's life.

Both a prayer and a petition need to cover essentially the same points:

1. The acknowledgment that Jesus Christ is the Son of God who died on the cross for our sins, as our substitute.
2. The acknowledgment that Jesus Christ rose from the dead to give us eternal life.
3. The acknowledgment by faith that Jesus Christ has forgiven us for our sins.

4. The acknowledgment that we are in a position to receive His presence into our lives and that we have the assurance of eternal life.

God's Word teaches us that we believe and then receive. A prayer or a confession needs to put a person in a position where he says, "I believe the gospel to be true. I receive Christ into my life."

The exact words used in a sinner's prayer or a confession can vary. God is most interested in the heart and in a willful surrender to Him.

Most assuredly, the time of prayer need not be long. I frequently have led a person into a spiritual birth experience with a prayer as short as this:

*Heavenly Father, have mercy upon me, a sinner. I accept right now what Your Son, Jesus Christ, did for me on the cross. Please forgive me of my sins. Fill me with Your presence, and give me your peace and joy. I receive Your promise of eternal life right now, and I ask You to fill me with Your Spirit so that I can be a totally new person on the inside. I pray this in Jesus' Name.*

## Can Such a Simple Time of Prayer Work?

Down through the years, people have said to me, "Such a simple prayer with a person isn't enough." One man said quite adamantly, "You mean to tell me that just by praying that simple prayer with that person—which took you no more than ninety seconds—you think the person is born again?"

Yes, I do. I see no evidence in Scripture where that is not the case.

I believe that the moment a person repents of his sins, invites Jesus Christ into his life, and receives God's forgiveness for his sins, that his eternal destiny is changed, he has a home in heaven, and he is spiritually birthed into God's kingdom.

That's the promise made by our Lord Himself in the most famous of all Bible verses: "For God so loved the world that He gave His only begotten Son, that whoever believes in Him should not perish but have everlasting life" (John 3:16).

Jesus didn't say that a person needed to complete a ten-week new converts class, or recite a long string of prayers or "I-believe" statements, or bow *x* number of times toward a shrine, or make a pilgrimage to a holy place—or even down the aisle to an altar—in order to be born anew. He said that when we *believe* in Him—which involves turning our backs on our old sinful ways and false beliefs, receiving forgiveness for those old beliefs, and turning toward a new way of believing and a new life in the Lord—we have *in that moment* a new destiny.

## Confessing Christ Is What's Important

Many times we believe that a person must bow his head, close his eyes, and pray a sinner's prayer in order to receive the Lord Jesus Christ into his life. There's no place in the Bible where that traditional formula is set forth as necessary. What the Bible does say is that "confessing" Jesus is Lord is the key to salvation.

Romans 10:9-10, 13 are particularly effective verses to read or quote:

> That if you confess with your mouth the Lord Jesus and believe in your heart that God has raised Him from the dead, you will be saved. For with the heart one believes unto righteousness, and with the mouth confession is made unto salvation. For whoever calls on the name of the LORD shall be saved.

If you are engaged in street witnessing in a rough section of town, the last thing anybody is interested in doing is bowing his head and closing his eyes. I found it an amazing discovery the day I learned that a person can accept Jesus into his life with his eyes open and his head up. In fact, I discovered people don't even need to fold their hands or address God in a formal prayer.

They can simply say, "Lord, I know I need you. Have mercy on me as a sinner. Please forgive me and set me free from guilt and sin. Make me a new creature in you, and give me Your peace."

Jesus promised, "Whoever confesses Me before men, him I will also confess before My Father who is in heaven" (Matthew 10:32).

## One Pastor's Experience: A Case Study

A pastor once shared the following story with me. He had been with me and two other men in a restaurant on a day four waitresses came to know the Lord. Upon experiencing first-hand what it meant to be involved in active soul winning, he made a firm commitment that he was going to engage in active soul winning at every possible opportunity. Here is what he told me:

The following Sunday after church, I was having lunch at a restaurant. A waitress walked up to our table, poured us a second cup of coffee, and I said to her, "You know, there's something encouraging that's happened to us at this table that you might be interested in knowing about. The Lord is at work in our lives. What is the Lord doing in your life?"

She looked at me and said, "Absolutely nothing and I don't care to hear about it."

I thought to myself, *Wow, what a beginning!*

Now at this particular steakhouse, the same waitress never seems to come to your table twice, so I watched for the next person the Lord might bring across my path. Sure enough, in a few minutes, a different waitress came to check on the coffee level in our cups, and I shared a little with her. She said, "Yes, I've accepted the Lord, but I just don't seem to have the time to do all the things I want to do—like go to church regularly or get involved in a group of Christians."

I said to her very gently, "You know, you seem to need some encouragement today, and perhaps that's why the Lord sent us here." I didn't take my eyes off her as I continued to share, "You need to have the Word of God established firmly in your life." I offered her the opportunity to fill out a card with her name and address so I could send her some more information about God's Word and to invite her to attend our church. She took the card, filled it out, brought it back to me before we left, and seemed extremely grateful that the opportunity was before her to grow in the Lord. She had accepted the Lord into her life two years before, and she said I was the first person who had encouraged her walk with the Lord since that initial new-birth experience!

## How About an Opportunity to Reject?

The pastor continued his story:

The next day, I drove into the gas station I usually frequent, and I saw the owner of the station standing inside. I felt convicted that

I had never shared Christ with this man, even though I had seen him and talked to him dozens of times through the years. The service station owner knew I was a pastor and knew the name of the church where I served, and I knew his name. And yet, the name of Jesus had never been raised between us.

This day I felt the Holy Spirit prompting me to take a different tactic. I got out of my car and, as I began to pump gas at the self-service pump, the service station owner came over to me. I greeted him warmly and then said, "Doug, when are you finally going to turn your life over to the Lord Jesus Christ?"

He stood there for a few minutes and started to argue, raising first one objection and then another. I quietly kept pumping gas into my car, and then I responded, "It's not the starving people in Africa, Doug. It's not the abused children. It's not the priest who rebuked you forty-five years ago. It's Jesus I'm talking to you about." The man became silent.

I said, "You know, Doug, if you want to reject Jesus, I should also give you that opportunity today. If you accept Him, you accept Him and confess Him publicly as a part of being saved. But if you choose to reject Him, you should also reject Him publicly."

This put the situation in an entirely different light for this service station owner. He wasn't ready to say, "I reject Jesus." Instead he responded, "I'll think about it."

Why did I take that approach? Well, the thought came to me that someday I might pull into this service station and not find this man. Or, perhaps something would happen to me so that I never came to this service station again. How could I explain to the Lord that I had encountered a man several dozen times in my life and yet had never mentioned His name to him and had never given him an opportunity to reject or accept Jesus Christ?

This is a good thought for each one of us to ponder as we recall the people we see again and again and again as we take in clothes to be dry-cleaned, have our hair cut, take our shoes to be repaired, stop in for food at the quick-stop place, and so forth. You know your routine. You know which people you see over and over.

- Consider your neighbors.
- Consider your children's teachers.
- Consider the professionals you consult periodically— your physician, attorney, CPA.

At some point, shouldn't you have the courage to say, "You know, I've been coming to you all these years, and I don't know if I've ever told you about the most important experience in my life." Share briefly with the person what Jesus means to you. Conclude, "I'd be making a big mistake, I think, if I didn't give you an opportunity to receive the Lord Jesus into your life, too."

What do you have to lose? A true professional is going to continue to serve you as her client or patient and is going to respect your straightforward, honest approach to sharing sincerely something that is vitally important to you. The clerk in a store is going to continue to wait upon you. Even if the person doesn't respond in the way you hope he will respond, you will know that should he ever need to talk to someone about the Lord, he'll know at least one Christian to whom he can turn.

What does the other person have to lose? Possibly his soul.

## Back to the Steakhouse

By the way, this pastor who became an active soul-winner and I went back to that steakhouse a couple of nights later and had an opportunity to talk to the cashier as we were paying our bill.

She said to me, "Where are you from?"

I said, "I'm from Tennessee. Could you tell that I'm not from around here?"

She said, "Yes, I really like your accent."

Not many people say that, so I proceeded, "Well, there's something you'd like even more about me if you knew it."

She said, "What's that?"

I said, "The Lord Jesus Christ lives within me." I shared a little further with her about the gospel and the fact that Jesus would like to live inside her, too, and forgive her and give her His spirit of peace, joy, and an assurance about her eternal future.

We prayed together and then, sure enough, other customers came toward her to pay their bills as soon as we were finished. I stepped to one side to wait until they were gone so I could get her name and address in order to send her some follow-up literature.

She got about halfway through writing her name and address when a man came up to pay his bill. I said, "You might be interested in knowing that Mary Jo just received the Lord Jesus into her life. Have you received the Lord into your life?"

He said, "No, but I'm just on the verge."

That was the first time anyone had said that to me! I figured being "just on the verge" is pretty much equal to being "ready"!

I said, "Well, the reason you're on the verge is because today is the day of salvation for you. So why don't you just go ahead and receive the Lord into your life." And Mary Jo, the pastor, Gerald (the man on the verge) and I prayed together, huddled there at the cashier's desk. Then Gerald filled out a card with his name and address, too.

One "no," one encouragement opportunity with a believer, one left questioning, and two accepts—not a bad "first week" of active soul winning for this pastor!

## Sealing a Decision

One morning as I was in my hotel room making some calls, the maid came to clean the room. As she was working, I began to tell her why I was in town—for a conference on Christian broadcasting. I said, "You know, Christ means everything to me. He died on the cross to pay for the forgiveness of my sins, and then He rose from the dead and He's alive today. He has sent His Holy Spirit to fill my life and give me a new heart and peace with God. The greatest, most encouraging thing that ever happened to me was when I received the Lord Jesus Christ into my life." She didn't say anything, just kept doing her work. I could tell, however, that she was listening to every word.

I went on, "You know, the really great thing is that it's so easy to receive the Lord into your life. All you have to do is call upon Him and say, 'Lord, have mercy upon me a sinner. Please forgive me of my sins, and come and dwell in my heart.'" She finished her work, and as she prepared to leave the room, I said, "You can do that, you know, at any time you want. If you want to receive Jesus into your life, you just need to call upon Him, no matter where you are."

She left the room.

As I left the room a few minutes later to go to the next seminar on my schedule, I saw her in the hallway. She had a glow on her face that she hadn't had when she was working in my room. I said, "You did what I told you to do, didn't you?" She said a bit bashfully, "Yeah."

"Did Christ come into your heart?"

She said, "Yes."

"Do you feel or sense that there's anything different in you?"

"Yes," she said. I asked her a couple of further questions to confirm to her, and to myself, that she had, indeed, confessed Jesus as the Savior and Lord of her life.

Later, during the convention, I led her in an opportunity to confess openly before several of her co-workers what the Lord had done in her life. She truly had been born anew in her spirit.

## Rejoicing with Grateful Hearts

People who come to the Lord may not know how to thank you. Sometimes all they can do is smile. Sometimes the emotions are too deep for words. Don't feel you need to linger in conversation.

One cab driver said to me, "I woke up this morning with a lot of problems on my mind." I took his comment as an open door for sharing the gospel, and during the course of our drive to my next appointment, he received Christ into his life. As we reached my destination and I started to get out of the cab, he said, "God sent you; I believe that! I feel a warmth inside me. He is doing something." I offered to send him a Bible, but he said, "I have one and I'm going to start reading it tonight." As I attempted to pay the fare, he said, "This is on me. You've made this a special day."

Rarely can a person express his or her thanks in a tangible way, and we shouldn't expect it. That's the only free cab ride I've ever received!

What we can do is rejoice with the person who has just received Christ. We can give a word of encouragement, words of follow-up or referral (see chapter 13), and then move on.

"God bless you and keep you" is a phrase that's been used by Christians for centuries as a parting greeting. So is, "May the Lord make His face to shine upon you always." You'll find through experience the most comfortable "benediction" for you to use. Leave the person with a positive, upbuilding word.

## And If a Person Turns You Down . . .

Don't take it personally.

Don't let it discourage you.

Don't let it keep you from speaking the name of Jesus to someone else.

Do take it as a sign from the Lord about what He would have you do for that person: *Pray!*

Pray that the Holy Spirit would bind the forces of spiritual darkness that are keeping that person blind to the truth.

Pray that the Holy Spirit would have dominion over the enemy that was keeping him deaf, spiritually speaking, to the message of the gospel.

Pray that the Holy Spirit might take authority over the principalities and powers that are keeping this person imprisoned and shut away in dungeons of despair and that the Holy Spirit would bring into the person's life those who might lead him to light.

Again, leave the person with a positive word. "May you come to know Him someday" is one phrase you might use. Or perhaps, "God loves you."

Let the last words the person hears from you be ones that are filled with the Lord's kindness and mercy—whether he accepts or rejects the Lord.

# ELEVEN

# SEIZING THE OPPORTUNITY, MAXIMIZING THE MOMENT

A few months ago, I came out of a hotel restaurant to find a woman from the hotel's maintenance staff kneeling on the sidewalk, scraping up bubble gum. I put my hand on her shoulder and said, "You know, while you're on your knees, this would be a good time for you to repent of your sins and to receive the Lord Jesus Christ into your heart. He's ready to come into your life and forgive your sins. You know you need that, don't you?"

She looked up at me a bit surprised and then said sincerely, "Yes, I do."

I said, "Well, let's just have prayer." And we prayed together right there.

The man I was with thought this was all very strange. He said, "Wow, I've never seen *that* before."

I said, "Neither have I! But it happened, didn't it?"

I was just as excited as he was over what had happened. And that's always the case. It's never commonplace to me that a person accepts the Lord. Each new soul born into the kingdom is precious. That person's spiritual new birth is a real miracle, and each case is distinctive, wonderful, awesome, and unique.

## Share from Your Present Moment

You may want to use your recent attendance or participation in a Christian seminar or church service as a take-off point in opening a conversation with someone.

A number of years ago, I participated in a Bible-reading seminar in Lanham, Maryland. After one of the sessions, three men and I went to a restaurant across the street for lunch. When the waitress came to our table, I asked her name and then said, "Well, Marty, these men and I are visiting the Bible college across from here to attend a seminar, and we're all real hungry. By the way, do you ever read the Bible?"

She said with hesitation, "Maybe a little." She left the menus and went away. When she returned, I tried to pick up the previous conversation as if no time had passed, "You know, the Bible contains a lot of great information about God and His church and how to have a personal relationship with God. Do you ever go to church?"

She said, "Well, I used to go, but not now." She took our orders and left.

When she returned to bring us our food, I picked up the conversation again. I said, "You know, going to church is important, but the most important thing is to have a personal one-on-one relationship with the Jesus of the Bible. Have you ever thought about that?"

She said, "I guess I'm not sure what you mean."

When she said that, I realized she only needed a little more information about the Lord. When she brought us a second round of coffee, I said, "Don't you think that if God is real and wants to have fellowship with those He has created, we ought to allow Him to do so by accepting His offer of salvation through His Son Jesus?"

She said, "I guess, but how do you do something like that, anyway?" I said, "It's really easy to receive Jesus. You can accept Him into your life right here. You don't have to pray on your knees. In fact, I know some people who have received the Lord in some of the strangest places."

I quoted Romans 10:9–10 to her and said, "Do you believe those verses from the Word of God?" She said, "I guess."

"Do you believe Jesus is the Son of God, who died on the cross for your sins?"

She said, "Yes." The other men at the table seemed a bit shocked at the realization that someone was about to be born into the kingdom!

I said, "Well, Marty, if you'll declare these verses, then Jesus will save you, right here and now. All you need to do is repeat these verses after me." I rephrased Romans 10:9–10 in this way:

"I confess that I am a sinner."
*"I confess that I am a sinner."*

"I confess Jesus is my Savior—"
*"I confess Jesus is my Savior—"*

"That He died on the cross for my sins."
*"That He died on the cross for my sins."*

"I believe in my heart that God has raised Jesus from the dead so I can have eternal life."
*"I believe in my heart that God has raised Jesus from the dead so I can have eternal life."*

I then gave her several additional words of encouragement about receiving the Lord into her life—with all of the joy and peace He had to give her—and about reading the Bible for herself, talking to God every day, and attending a church regularly so she could hear the Word of God preached. The men at the table all rose to shake her hand.

One of the other waitresses in the restaurant stopped to see what all the commotion was about. I said, "Marty just received Jesus Christ as her personal Savior and Lord, something that will change her life forever since her sins have now been forgiven."

I looked at Marty and said, "Isn't that right?"

She said, "Yes, that's right!" I asked the second waitress, "Wouldn't you like to experience that, too? Knowing your sins are forgiven and you have a personal relationship with God to help you through this life?" She said, "Yes, I would."

Not only were the lives of these two waitresses changed

that day, but also the lives of the three men with whom I was having lunch. I've heard from each of them, through the years, and each of them felt a new release in his spirit that day about witnessing and openly sharing the Lord Jesus with others.

One of them, my friend Ken Boaz, has made active soul winning the focal point of his life—both through his part-time teaching at a college and in his work as an entrepreneur and businessman.

# Be Present in a Time of Crisis

One of the most fertile fields in which to share the gospel is a hospital. I have found this to be especially true in visiting those who are facing surgery the following morning.

Go early in the evening, after all of the pre-operative tests have been made and before the person has been given a sedative for the night. Take your Bible with you. Ask the nurses to direct you to rooms where patients are facing next-day surgery; you might share the gospel with them, too.

If the person you meet in a hospital room is a Christian, he'll be delighted to have you pray with him for a successful surgery. If the person isn't a believer, she is usually delighted to have someone pray with her, too!

"Hello, my name is Jerry, and the Lord Jesus Christ has sent me here tonight to tell you that God loves you. He is concerned about every part of your being and about the surgery you are facing tomorrow. He's concerned about your spiritual destiny, too."

The Christian will nearly always respond at that point and let you know she is a believer. Ask if you can pray with her for God's wisdom to be with her surgeon and for God's healing power to bring her to a full recovery. I've never had a believer refuse such an offer of prayer.

If the person isn't a believer, you can nearly always tell by the look on his face. Often, tears will well up in his eyes at hearing the news that God loves him and is concerned about him.

"You've been thinking a lot more about spiritual things

lately, haven't you?" Nearly every person I've met who is facing a major illness or surgery has been thinking more about his spiritual state of affairs.

"Before you face this surgery tomorrow, wouldn't you like to know that things are settled in your soul between you and God? You can do that right now by accepting the sacrifice that Jesus made on the cross for you, by repenting of your sinful ways, and by receiving Jesus into your life. He'll not only give you the assurance of eternal life, but He'll give you His peace and joy as you face this surgery. We can pray right now if you'd like."

If the person does not respond positively to you, you can offer to pray for his safe surgery, and before you leave his room, you can say, "I want you to know that you can call upon the Lord all by yourself, at any time of the day or night. Perhaps when you are alone later tonight you'll want to invite the Lord into your life."

A gently spoken, loving invitation to receive Christ is nearly always accepted by an unbeliever in these moments.

"But," you may say, "does such a conversion really last?"

Again, that's the concern of the Holy Spirit. If the person does accept the Lord, you can say, "When you are back on your feet, you'll want to find a church and get involved with a group of people who are learning and applying the Word of God to their lives. But even before then, you can read the Bible as you rest and recuperate. You can talk to God and pour out your feelings and thoughts to Him, any time of the day or night, wherever you are. Ask Him for His help every day."

I once had a man say to me, "Foxhole conversions don't last."

I said, "How do you know?"

"Well," he said, "people say things in the heat of the moment and then when everything is fine, they forget what they said."

I said, "That may be true for some people, but I don't believe it's true for everyone. Are you saying that we shouldn't share Christ with people who are facing an emergency or a crisis in their lives?"

He was silent.

I went on, "If that's the case, we probably shouldn't share Christ with anyone, because just about everybody I know is facing an emergency or a crisis, or they just got over one, or a new one is just around the corner. Life is a series of emergencies and crises."

He said, "Well, that's true."

I concluded, "What if the person dies on the operating table? Are they any less saved because they accepted the Lord the night before than if they had accepted Him thirty years ago? The Lord gave a parable specifically about that, in which He taught that those who were hired into the field at the last hour were paid the same wages as those who had worked all day. Is the person who accepts Christ in a foxhole any less saved if he is killed in the battle?"

Again, the issue is not really ours to determine or to control. The Holy Spirit, who brought you to that room and the person to that point of decision, will also bring growth.

The Holy Spirit doesn't abandon His newborn babes in Christ.

I've talked with a number of people through the years who say to me, "Well, I once called upon God during a particularly bad time in my life, but that probably doesn't count since I haven't paid much attention to Him since things got better."

I always respond, "If you genuinely trusted the Lord, it *does* count. And you can renew your relationship with the Lord right now so that you can grow in your faith and realize more of what God has for you."

Never discount a spiritual birth experience. Don't negate, dismiss, or downplay a spiritual conversion encounter. Spiritual birth is God's work. Furthermore, it's a work in process that can only be evaluated from heaven's vantage point and the perspective of eternity.

# Be Present Even After the Altar Call

Sometimes a person will feel an urge to respond to the pastor's invitation to receive the Lord at the close of a church service but will not go forward. In conversing with people after the service has ended, you might give them another opportunity.

One evening my family was invited to a pastor's home after an evening service. People were engaging in casual conversation, greeting old friends, and getting acquainted. I began to speak with one woman about the service and noticed that she seemed quiet and a bit troubled. I said, "There's something troubling you, isn't there? Was it something that happened during the service?"

She admitted that some of the things the pastor had said had troubled her—in a convicting way. I shared several thoughts with her from the Word of God and then asked her, "When the pastor gave the invitation to go forward, you wanted to go, didn't you?"

She said, "Yes, I did. But I just couldn't seem to get up enough courage to walk down that aisle."

I said, "Well, you can receive the Lord into your life right now."

"Here?" she asked.

"Yes. The Lord looks on your heart, not your surroundings."

I put my hand on her shoulder and we prayed right there, with everyone around us continuing to carry on their conversations as before. They didn't even seem to notice what had happened. The woman, however, was greatly changed. Her countenance of reserve and fear became one of brightness and joy.

I introduced her to several people there, saying, "Linda has some exciting news to tell you" or, "Have you heard the good news about Linda?" Most people assumed she had walked forward to receive Christ as her Savior during the service. It didn't matter that she hadn't. What did matter was that she came to know the Lord. She was later baptized in that church and became a faithful member.

## A God-Created Stable for Birth

Can a person accept the Lord Jesus while standing behind a cash register at a cafe?

Why not?

There's nothing in the Scriptures that says people need to be in any particular location or position in order to send forth a sincere cry of repentance from the heart and to open their lives to the redemptive work of Christ Jesus.

One of the things I've found to be true as I've shared Christ in public places is that the Holy Spirit will create a divine "altar" of space around a person if, indeed, it is that person's time to be born anew spiritually.

For example, I once noted that a cashier had been busy for nearly an hour, taking money and credit cards from a seemingly unending string of customers. Yet, no one was at the counter when I paid my bill. I took that as my cue to share the Lord with her. It was as if I had entered a cocoon of divine space that no one else could penetrate for a few moments.

During the entire time I conversed and prayed with this cashier who received the Lord, and during the time it took me to write her address so I could send her follow-up information no one came toward the cash register area. Not a waiter or waitress. Not a customer. No one came into the restaurant from outside to be seated. We were alone, or so it seemed, in a place set apart from the rest of the world.

When the time comes for a person to be born again, the Holy Spirit creates a space for that birth to take place. It is a quiet, holy, set-apart moment in the person's life. I like to think of it as a stable, of sorts. Just as the Holy Spirit created a place for Mary to give birth to the baby Jesus, so the Holy Spirit creates a private out-of-the-traffic-flow space for Jesus to be born yet again, this time in a person's life.

I knew this to be true in a special way the day I discovered . . .

# A Grocery Store Is as Good a Place as Any to Receive the Lord!

I went to a grocery store not too long ago to pick up a few items. My son Jonathan was with me, and by the time we got to the front of the check-out line, I was surprised to notice that no one was standing in line behind us.

Again, I saw this "space" as a cue from the Lord that He might be seeking to bring someone to a new-birth experience, and so I said to my son, "I'm going to share the Lord with this person. You pray quietly in your spirit and stay close."

I noticed the woman's name badge, looked her in the eye, and shared with her, "Regina, you've probably been thinking more lately about the Lord and wondering if He has anything special for you, haven't you?" She responded with a smile. I went on to share with her briefly, but directly, that the Lord loved her and had died on the cross for her sins, and that today was a good day for her to accept what the Lord had done for her, to turn her back on the past sins of her life, to receive God's forgiveness, and to be freed of guilt and experience the peace and joy God had for her.

She nodded and said, again with a big smile, "Yes, I know I need that."

And so we prayed together—right there at the check-out stand—as she finished sacking the few items we had purchased. No one came to the check-out line with groceries while we talked and prayed. As soon as we finished, along came several people with carts piled high.

As I left Regina standing at her cash register, I noticed a man and a boy sitting on a bench near the entrance. I stopped and touched the man on the shoulder and said, "You might be interested in knowing that the woman standing at that check-out line, Regina, just received Jesus Christ into her heart and experienced the forgiveness of her sins."

He had a sober look on his face. I went on, "You need to do that, too, don't you?" He nodded and said, "Yes, I do." And so I prayed with him and shared with him a little more about the Lord. I noticed that the boy sitting next to him—whom I learned was his stepson, Kerry—had been watching and listening intently. I turned to him and said, "And you need to experience this salvation miracle, too, don't you?" He said yes. After I finished praying with Kerry, the man shared with me that his wife didn't know the Lord. So I told him briefly how to tell her about Jesus and how to pray with her.

As it turned out, this man's wife made her way through the

check-out stand just as we were finishing our conversation, and the man introduced his wife to me. I said, "You might be interested in knowing that your husband and your son have just invited Jesus Christ into their hearts. You need to do that too, don't you?" She also said yes, and I led her to the Lord and prayed with her.

My son and I went to pick up a few groceries. God had in mind that we went to rescue a few souls and add them to the kingdom.

I never cease to be amazed at how God fulfills His Word, which says, "The steps of a good man are ordered by the LORD; / And He delights in his way" (Psalm 37:23). Trust God to order your steps. Expect that God will place someone along your path, and will direct you to take certain paths, so that souls will be there, "white unto harvest."

## A String of Won Souls

The first thing I try to do after I've led someone to the Lord is to get that person to share the faith with someone else. I do this for three reasons.

First, God Word says:

Whoever confesses that Jesus is the Son of God, abides in him, and he in God (1 John 4:15).

And again,

If you confess with your mouth the Lord Jesus and believe in your heart that God has raised Him from the dead, you will be saved. For with the heart one believes unto righteousness, and with the mouth confession is made unto salvation (Romans 10:9–10).

When a person confesses his new relationship in Christ Jesus to someone else, that relationship is sealed within his heart.

Second, an immediate confession of Christ Jesus imprints the life of the new believer with the concept of soul winning. The brand-new Christian tends to be exuberant, glowing, radiant, and joy-filled. He is rarely intimidated at the prospect of sharing this new-found peace and joy with others. Brand-new Christians are ideal witnesses, to a great extent because they have not yet been taught by other Christians how scary or daunting the prospect of witnessing can be! If a person is able to lead another person to Christ within a relatively short time after his own conversion, he will be far less intimidated by the idea of sharing his faith with others in the future. He'll be much more likely to go home and share the good news of what has happened to him with his family and friends.

Third, the brand-new Christian is the prime example to the nonbeliever of how Christ can change a life. He is an immediate example of a "before and after" conversion story. The new Christian also portrays to the unbeliever, as no one else can, that a relationship with Christ is not only possible, but easy to enter into.

I have often led four or five people to the Lord in this sequential manner, using the conversion of one person to witness to another. In fact, at times, I've even stopped total strangers on the street to say, "Hey, guess what just happened to this man! He's been born again and is full of joy. Did you know you can be, too?"

By the way, when sharing with someone who is at work, it's very important to be sensitive to the value of his time and not to distract him from his job. The noon rush hour at a restaurant is not the time, for example, to attempt to engage a waitress in a discussion about the gospel. I often order my day so I am eating at restaurants during "off" hours—when I can share more openly and in a more relaxed way with a waitress or waiter, cashier, or other customers who might also be stopping in for a snack or beverage.

People tend to work or associate in clusters. Take, for example, a team of maids that works together in a hotel. If you have the opportunity to lead one of them to the Lord, you'll probably find that it's a fairly easy matter to gather several of the other maids on that floor together to share the good news. Joy radiates. Smiles are contagious. Good news travels only slightly slower than bad news, and when the good news is the gospel, it sometimes travels faster!

The person who has received Christ is probably known to his or her co-workers. They can readily see a change in the person's life and are usually very willing to share in the person's newfound joy, even if they aren't ready to accept Christ in their own lives. If the person's co-worker is already a believer, there will usually be great rejoicing that a colleague has come to know the Savior, and this shared joy frequently draws the attention of—and is attractive to—other co-workers.

I've also encountered situations in which a co-worker of the new believer is a "backslidden Christian"—a person who has had a relationship with the Lord in the past, but who hasn't communicated with the Lord in a long time. The new believer's conversion experience is an ideal time to lead that person into a renewal of his commitment to Christ. Frequently, the renewed believer becomes a much more active soul winner after such an experience—perhaps, in part, because he feels a little guilty that he never shared the gospel with his co-worker before.

When people come to Christ in clusters, each new believer in the group has her relationship with Christ reinforced. Co-workers can share the Bible, encourage, admonish, and help build up one another.

After leading several co-workers to the Lord, I suggest to them that they each get a copy of the New Testament, read it, and share it with one another as a part of their working day. I have prayer with them as a group and encourage them also to pray for and with one another as problems or questions arise. Nothing ties new converts together as much as talking about the Lord and the Scriptures and praying together.

Not only do I ask a new believer to share the news of his spiritual birth with another person, but I use that news in my next witnessing experience.

*My* faith is strengthened as I do this. And, the opportunity is nearly always there to share the good news that Jesus is Savior and Lord before the joy I feel has had a chance to diminish. It's much easier to share with a person—"Guess what just happened? That woman over there just received Jesus Christ as her Savior and has been made a new creature, forgiven of her sins and having eternal life. Isn't that great news?"—and to do so with an infectious enthusiasm, if you are sharing the news within seconds of the person's being born anew.

There's a joy of spirit that comes when a new name is written in the Lamb's Book of Life—the Bible even says that all of heaven rejoices in that moment! This joy is contagious and perhaps the most effective witness of all.

I once said to a cashier, "That person over there just accepted Jesus Christ over lunch. Isn't that great! God is doing so many encouraging things."

Now, all you have to do is look in a person's eyes when you make a statement like that to see what you should say or do next. Tears came into the cashier's eyes. I said, "Would you like to experience that, too? You can, you know. We can pray right now, since there's nobody standing in line to pay a bill."

She nodded and I had her repeat a simple prayer after me. I feel certain that anyone who may have been watching us from across the room would have thought we were huddled over my bill trying to see if the waiter had added the numbers correctly. In fact, we were conducting heaven's business. Her tears in that moment were tears of joy.

I wish you could have seen her smile!

# WORKING WITH A SUPPORT TEAM

The more you engage in active soul winning, the more you will find yourself sharing your experiences with others. You'll be eager to say, "Guess what just happened? Let me tell you how the Lord worked. You won't believe it, but . . . ."

The joy of winning a person to the Lord will fill you to over-flowing, and you'll find that you can hardly wait to tell your fellow Christians about people who received the Lord into their lives.

As you share with others the results of your active witness, and as they hear you giving the credit to the Lord for preparing the hearts and for forgiving sins, they'll be encouraged to be more bold in their witnessing. A desire to be an active soul winner will be birthed in them.

As they actively share their faith and see souls saved, still other Christians will be encouraged and made bold.

Can the church end up with too many soul winners?

No!

Not until the entire world is evangelized. And, believe me, that's still a distant goal.

When you become part of a group of people who not only take soul winning seriously, but who become committed to engaging in active soul winning at every opportunity, you'll find that you draw strength and boldness from that association. Your sharing of experiences will lead you to new insights in winning souls more effectively. You may want to go out in teams of two to cafes, bus stops, or other public places to "fish" for souls.

It is vitally important for you always to . . .

## Stay in Fellowship with Other Believers

The Lord never called us to walk this path alone.

The Lord is the one who said we are to be His "body," with each member fitted to the next so that the entire body can be whole.

The Lord is the one who devised the means by which the Holy Spirit gives different gifts and abilities to various ones for the building up of the whole.

In order to stay fueled to speak to others boldly about the Lord, you must stay in fellowship with other believers—especially with those who share your interest in seeing others receive Jesus Christ into their lives. If you don't, it's easy to become discouraged, and you may soon feel as if the entire world is against your Savior.

In your association with a group that is committed to seeing souls saved, you'll also . . .

- gain a great deal of insight as you learn new approaches to try,
- gain strength from prayer times in which you join your hearts together in asking the Lord to prepare you and to prepare others for a spiritual new-birth experience,
- and have an opportunity to practice sharing your testimony with others.

If an active soul-winner group isn't available for you to join, prayerfully consider starting such a group within your church or Bible study group.

As your group's witness in your community becomes more widespread, you may find that you will meet a person who says, "You know, a man just told me about the Lord a few days ago." If the person has not yet received the Lord into his life, your witness is one more opportunity for him to do so. If he has, you have a prime opportunity to encourage him in the Lord.

# We All Learn Best by Doing

You can read this book a dozen times, take five seminars in soul-winning techniques, hear a dozen tape series on how to witness, and you'll still find that the best, most efficient, and most rewarding way to learn how to lead a person to the Lord is by doing.

A man once asked me if he could go with me wherever I went for a few days to see if what I had taught at a conference on soul winning really worked. He wanted to see soul winning in action. This man said, "I'm a pastor, but I don't know how to win souls like you do." He did go with me, and he learned how to become an active soul winner in the process.

During the 1984 Olympics, a young Christian worker who was helping us with the media staff told me with sorrow in her voice that she had not led anyone to the Lord in the past year. I invited her to come with me to distribute some literature that Bible Pathway Ministries had prepared specifically for the Olympic games. That day she led two people to Christ!

Soul winning is easier if you're working alongside someone who is as eager to see people come to the Lord as you are.

As a part of the personal evangelism seminars I have conducted from time to time, I ask those who are interested to join me in going to a public place to witness. It helps to see the principles of active soul winning in action!

One time, a friend of mine—journalist Bill Armstrong—and I were joined by four others from a seminar as we went to a shopping mall.

In the course of about forty-five minutes, we led four people to the Lord. In the first instance, I sat down by a Chinese lady who was sitting on a bench in the mall and I said, "My friends and I have discovered that more and more people are thinking about the Lord these days, and I'm wondering if you are someone who has been thinking more about God lately?"

She said, "Yes, as a matter of fact, I have been wondering about God lately."

I went on to share with her how she could receive the Lord Jesus into her life and experience the peace of mind and joy that comes from knowing one's sins are forgiven. As I finished praying with her, I noticed a man sitting on the other side of her and I said, "Excuse me, you might be interested in knowing that Ann, here, has just received the Lord Jesus Christ into her life. Has that ever happened to you?"

He said, "No, it hasn't."

I said, "Well, you'd like to be forgiven of your sins and know that you had a personal relationship with the Lord, wouldn't you?"

He said yes, and I went on to share with him and pray with him.

Meanwhile, across the mall, Bill and the two people he was with were having similar experiences.

What a great time we had rejoicing at the close of that hour! Not only had four new souls been birthed into the kingdom by the Holy Spirit, but four new soul winners had been set on fire, too!

## Teams Can Have Varied Approaches

The evangelism team you choose may be a short-term team gathered for a specific event. Some 11,000 people from around the world, plus several thousand local believers, gathered to be part of just such an effort at the 1984 Olympic Games in Los Angeles. These people distributed *The Winning Way* (Gospel of John) produced by Bible Pathway Ministries, which was printed in nine languages.

Another outreach during the Olympic Games was initiated by a printer in the Los Angeles area who donated bus posters that read, "For Peace, Talk to Jesus." They were printed in Chinese, Spanish, and English. Another 500 signs posted inside the buses showed a photo of Calvin Smith, U.S. Olympic gold medal champion in track, with a heading that said, "I gave my life to Jesus Christ. You can give your life to Jesus, too." The poster included John 3:15 and a telephone number.

The people themselves gave away the Lord within them in ways that were varied and distinctive.

- Children performed skits and sang songs about Jesus in nearby parks.
- A drama troupe presented the gospel in pantomime.
- A young man who was a former gang member told his story on street corners.

Each group, each subgroup, each team, each person, presented Jesus in a unique way. It was a truly amazing phenomenon to watch as the Holy Spirit orchestrated this mass outreach to people from so many nations, both athletes and spectators.

The most amazing thing to me was that the object of their witness was the same: to lead people to receive the Lord in a personal way.

Later, I reflected that from the Lord's vantage point in heaven, each day is a day of mobilizing His evangelism team on this earth. Each day, the Holy Spirit holds an agenda of arranging unbelievers to cross the paths of believers. He speaks. He woos. He draws. He compels. He arranges schedules, encounters, times, places, people, personalities, experiences, and backgrounds for one supreme purpose: to draw lost men and women to a relationship with Jesus Christ so that they might experience God's power in their lives now and live with the Lord forever.

If a large convention or group is coming to your city, make plans to mingle with the crowd. Only one thing can put a stop to the Lord's sovereign work in setting up appointments for souls to be won. It's our unwillingness to open our mouths and share the name of Jesus.

# Expect to Be Built Up as a Body of Believers

When we witness to others about the Lord, not only are we sharing the gospel, bringing people into the kingdom, and planting seeds that the Holy Spirit can grow into an eternal harvest. No, still more is at work. The very process is transforming *us* into the likeness of Jesus.

Nothing makes you more like Jesus than participating in ongoing, active soul winning.

It's through a desire and an obedience in active soul winning that you put yourself in a position to be directed by the Holy Spirit, just as Jesus was.

It's through seeking to be an active soul winner that you put yourself in a position to do only what you see the Father doing, and to speak only what the Father compels you to speak—which is just the way Jesus said He lived. He came to seek and to save the lost.

It's through your speaking His Word and sharing His truth with others that the Word of God and the truth of the gospel become imprinted on your soul. This process literally transforms you from who you were as a flesh-only creation to who you can be as a whole man or woman in Christ Jesus.

It's through your boldness and courage in speaking the name of Jesus that you grow and are empowered to have dominion and authority over evil spirits that come against the work of God.

Active soul winning brings the lost to Christ. It also brings us, as Christians, into a more intimate fellowship with Him!

We may think—usually with a little smugness and pride—that we are doing something for God when we witness about Jesus.

The truth is that He is doing something through us and in us and for us, allowing us to take part in His divine drama for purposes higher than any we can imagine.

Winning souls not only builds up the kingdom of God, it builds you up. It keeps your faith alive. James 2:26 says, "For as the body without the spirit is dead, so faith without works is dead also." Sharing the gospel with people is the number one work we have before us.

## Pray Together as a Team and Expect Results

Jesus promised His followers, "Greater works than these he will do, because I go to My Father" (John 14:12). How is that possible? It certainly isn't possible because of who we are. Rather, it's because Jesus fully expected to continue to live His life through us. He fully intended that we experience the same quality of life that He experienced on this earth. He said He was sending the Holy Spirit to indwell us for just that purpose—to assure us that we could live in Him, even as He lives in us.

- Pray together as a team that God will use you as laborers in the harvest.
- Pray together as a team for lost souls.
- Pray together as a team that you will each be sensitive to the leading of the Holy Spirit and that your paths will be directed solely by Him.
- Pray together as a team for boldness.

And then, expect God to answer your prayers! Don't put a ceiling on how many souls you believe you can reach for the Lord. Only the Lord knows that.

When I'm on the road and around a lot of people, I find that I often lead from one to eight people a day to the Lord—rarely more than eight and usually at least one. That means I have from five to thirty or more conversations, and that seems to be the maximum in which I can engage and still keep the appointments on my schedule.

I don't know how the Lord will lead you or work through you. But I do know this, I believe you can lead *many* people to our Lord Jesus Christ.

Expect great things from the Lord. I'm still expecting more and more souls to be won. I'm never satisfied. I see no scriptural basis for our ever sitting back and saying, "Well, I've done my part for the Lord."

In fact, I can hardly wait until my next opportunity to share the good news about our Lord Jesus! I am even more excited to see that the Lord is raising up an army of effective personal witnesses. Certainly the fields are "white for harvest."

I also believe there will be an increased openness to the gospel in the days ahead.

# THIRTEEN

# REFERRALS AND FOLLOW-UPS

What a joy it is for us to know that we have been chosen by Christ and ordained that we should go and bring forth fruit, and that our fruit should remain! (See John 15:16.)

God desires people to "remain" as part of His kingdom even more than you do!

## God Won't Let Them Get Away

On a number of occasions, I've shared the gospel with a person and he has not responded. Then I've seen the person again several months later, and he has said, "You remember that you told me how to receive Christ?"

"Yes, I remember."

"Well, I did!"

The words shared with him—the good seed—finally germinated. The soil was finally ready for the seed, and what had been shared took root and grew.

God will not let people get away from what He has spoken to them.

Sometimes I leave people who reject what I have to say with these parting words: "The Lord will be confirming to your heart what I've been telling you about His love for you and His desire to forgive you. You can respond to the Lord on your own. You don't need to pray with me or with anyone else, but you can call upon the Lord wherever you are—even driving your car down the highway on your way to work—and He'll hear you. The Bible promises, 'Whoever calls on the name of the LORD shall be saved.' When you call upon

Him, you can be assured that He'll hear you and respond to you." (See Romans 10:13.)

# Don't Be Dissuaded

Don't allow anyone to convince you that you shouldn't lead people to the Lord because you aren't equipped to follow through personally and make certain that they are well-grounded in the gospel.

Your job as a soul winner is to birth souls.

Consider the situation of a midwife, or an obstetrician. The doctor or midwife delivers that baby. She didn't conceive it, didn't personally carry the child through the pregnancy, and didn't have anything to do with the growth of the baby in the mother's womb, except perhaps to provide information to the mother about how to eat correctly and lead a life conducive to bearing a healthy child. The role of the midwife or obstetrician is to bring the child from darkness to light, from the womb to the world. Your role as a soul winner is highly similar. Your job is to bring a child of God—who has been created in God's image, nurtured and wooed by the Holy Spirit to the place of birth—into the kingdom of God.

Furthermore, the midwife or obstetrician doesn't have the responsibility for raising the child. That is the role of the parents. The obstetrician, professionally speaking, quickly turns over even the medical responsibility for the infant to a pediatrician.

Your role, as one who helps people through spiritual birth, is to refer them to someone who can feed them the Word of God, teach them and train them in the ways of the Lord, encourage their inherent talents to be brought to fullness through the power of the Holy Spirit, and prepare them for spiritual warfare.

In my opinion, to say, "You shouldn't win a person to the Lord if you don't follow through" is an excuse for not winning souls. I strongly suggest to you that it's an excuse that doesn't hold water with the Lord. Your follow-through message can be as simple as this:

Now that you've received the Lord, you need to do three things. First, you need to get involved in a church where the Word of God is taught and preached with faith. Look for such a church until you find one, and then attend there regularly. It's important for your soul to be fed with spiritual food.

Second, you need to read your Bible every day. If you don't have a Bible, I'd like to send you one.

If the person is a new convert, I then suggest that he begin by reading the Gospel of John, Colossians, and 1 John. I also recommend the Bible Pathway plan of reading through the entire Bible every year. It takes fifteen minutes a day and is a method I've used for years.

And third, you need to talk to the Lord every day. Tell Him how you feel. Ask Him to help you live your new life. Ask Him to show you what to do and how to respond to others. Invite Him to work within your heart to make you more like Jesus.

What am I sharing with the person? The basics for every Christian—new or old.

1. Fellowship with other believers.
2. Daily read God's Word.
3. Spend time daily in prayer.

You can share this simple 1-2-3 follow-up plan with a person you lead to the Lord in less than sixty seconds.

It's up to the person to follow through. You can be assured that the Holy Spirit will be doing His part to protect the person and lead and guide him.

## Referring Those Who Receive Christ

A person who experiences a spiritual rebirth needs nourishment in order to grow strong in Christ. Being spiritually born anew is one thing. Maturing in the Lord is another.

Nurturing a person in Christ is the responsibility of a teacher or pastor.

The Bible speaks of five callings or types of work within the church.

And He Himself gave some to be apostles, some prophets, some evangelists, and some pastors and teachers, for the equipping of the saints for the work of ministry, for the edifying of the body of Christ, till we all come to the unity of the faith and of the knowledge of the Son of God, to a perfect man, to the measure of the stature of the fullness of Christ *(Ephesians 4:11–13)*.

The soul winner is an evangelist. An evangelist is one who proclaims the good news of Jesus Christ and brings people to the decision point of accepting Him as their personal Savior and Lord. We are all called to do the work of an evangelist.

Now, some of us are better at being evangelists than others. Usually that's through practice. Sometimes it comes as a special call of God on our lives. This same passage in Ephesians says, "To each one of us grace was given according to the measure of Christ's gift" (Ephesians 4:7). We all have Christ within us. We all have the ability to share our faith, to be led by the Holy Spirit, to lead another person in a prayer of repentance, and to see him come into a newness of life.

On occasion, critics have said to me, "It's wrong to bring people to a spiritual birth and not follow through with them."

Following through is not solely my responsibility, although I do it when possible. That is the role of the entire church, and usually of a person who is gifted and experienced as a pastor or teacher.

We trust the Holy Spirit to bring people to the point of being born anew. We must also trust the Holy Spirit to continue the process of spiritual growth. The Holy Spirit doesn't abandon a person the moment he accepts the Lord Jesus. That's when He can truly begin His work in their lives!

The Scriptures are clear on this point. "He who has begun a good work in you will complete it until the day of Jesus Christ" (Philippians 1:6). The Holy Spirit will continue to develop a person until the microsecond in which Jesus Christ returns to this earth or we die and find ourselves in glory with Him. Just as our birth comes about because of His wooing, so our growth continues as we submit our lives to His instruction.

Again the Scriptures declare, "He who calls you is faithful, who also will do it" (1 Thessalonians 5:24). The Holy Spirit is the one who gently and persistently calls us toward the Lord Jesus. He is also the one who gives us the ongoing ability to remain true to our relationship with the Lord and to do all the things described in the verses preceding that statement: to be at peace, to follow good, to rejoice evermore, to pray without ceasing, to give thanks in everything, to quench not the Spirit, to despise not prophesyings, to prove all things, to hold fast to that which is good, to abstain from all appearance of evil, and to come to the place where our whole spirit, soul, and body are preserved blameless unto the coming of the Lord Jesus Christ. Read 1 Thessalonians 5:11–24 and rejoice. Your growth in Christ Jesus is something the Holy Spirit desires for you even more than you desire it.

## Your Responsibility for a Person's Growth as a Soul Winner

Your primary responsibility as a person who leads others to Christ Jesus is twofold: to bring them to birth and to point them toward a place where they can receive nourishment.

I have traveled a great deal as the result of various employment and ministry opportunities I've had through the years, and I've made contacts with outstanding church leaders in virtually every city of this nation. When I lead a person to the Lord, I frequently refer them to a church that is led by one of my pastor friends.

When possible, I get the new convert's name, address, and telephone number, and then I ask someone I know in that area—either a pastor or layman in whom I have confidence—to follow up with the person.

You may not have these contacts, but you can always refer the person to a church in the area. Encourage the person to go to the pastor and to say, "I've repented of my sins and have accepted Jesus as my Lord." I don't know a genuine pastor of the faith who would do anything other than rejoice greatly at such news!

If you are speaking to a person in your own city, invite him to come to your church. Make an appointment to meet him at the front door on a specific day and at a specific time. Sit with him through the service. Afterwards, introduce him to the pastor and to some of your friends in the church. Let him tell what has happened to him. (This confession of faith will build up and encourage others.) Invite him to become part of a Sunday school class or a Bible study that focuses on the Word of God.

## Offering to Send the Person a Bible

In addition to referring people to a place where they can receive pastoral care and teaching of the Word, you can also make an effort to provide them with a Bible or New Testament.

If at all possible, I ask people if they'd be willing to give me their address so I can send them more information to help them in their walk with the Lord. You can usually purchase this material in bulk, at discounted prices, from ministries or through bookstores—especially if you talk to the manager and let him know how you are using the material. I've found that most Christian bookstore owners are eager to see people come to the Lord, and they are willing to give you a greatly reduced rate over the retail price of a New Testament when they realize you are using the New Testaments in a follow-up ministry. This is especially true if you order inexpensive Bibles in bulk.

I recommend versions of the Bible or New Testament that are in everyday modern English. These Bibles are much more readily understood by new believers.

One of the main reasons to encourage a new believer to get a Bible and read it is that the Holy Spirit will use the Scriptures to show that new babe in Christ just who Jesus is. The Scriptures teach. They speak of the Lord. They reveal Him.

Preachers and teachers are good. In many cases they are a shortcut to greater understanding. Christian books about the Bible are a great help. But the Scriptures are the ultimate authority on who Jesus is, and nothing takes their place.

## Using Literature as a Means of Follow-Up

In addition to volunteering to send a person a copy of the New Testament, I sometimes . . .

- Give a year's subscription to *Bible Pathway* or other Bible study materials.
- Use tracts. I nearly always have a few with me. I especially like the ones that are easy to read. *A Clean Heart, Eternal Life, Steps to Peace with God, A Full and Meaningful Life, The Bridge, Facts of Life, The Four Spiritual Laws,* and *The Winning Way* are among my favorites. They tell you right up front that they have information about how a person can experience something they want. I don't know a person who wouldn't like a clean heart, eternal life, or more meaning and purpose in life.

I also keep a supply of the Gospel of John with me as I travel. In my opinion, the best follow-up literature you can give to a new convert is a copy of the complete Gospel of John.

If you offer to send a person a Bible or New Testament, follow through as quickly as you can. Just as a newborn infant can't be left without food for very long without starving to death, so a new believer needs to have access to spiritual nourishment as quickly as possible.

## Check Out Local Churches

You may discover, as I have, that many people you lead to the Lord speak a language other than English. I have found in recent years that a great many Spanish-speaking people are coming to know the Lord. There's a little-publicized, but very real, revival taking place among Spanish-speaking people across our land, and many are ready to accept the Lord as their personal Savior and Lord. Following up with a New Testament written in Spanish is important.

Within your own city, you may want to call upon, visit

with, or at least gain basic information about some of the churches that present the gospel in other languages. Familiarize yourself with them so you can refer new believers to them. Los Angeles, for example, is a city with a number of churches that regularly hold services in Chinese, Korean, Vietnamese, Spanish, and just about any other major language you can name!

## Go Back for Repeated Visits

As I travel to various cities in the course of my work, I am always on the look-out for people I've led to the Lord. I tend to stay in the same hotel in any given city, which provides me an opportunity to follow up personally with some whom I've led to the Lord, and also to introduce new people to the Lord by way of asking about those with whom I've shared in the past.

Once I've led a person to the Lord in a particular restaurant, I usually try to go back to that place as many times as I can during my stay in a city. I find that as one person in that group tells another about what happened, others become interested and are more ready to hear the gospel. The result is sometimes a domino effect.

I recently returned to a restaurant where I had led two waitresses and a waiter to the Lord several months earlier. I said to my waitress, "I was here last October, and I had the opportunity to share with a couple of waitresses at that time who received Christ into their hearts. Do you know them, or do you know if they still work here?"

Most restaurants have a high turnover rate and the waitress I asked didn't know the young women with whom I had shared the previous year. However, my question did open the door to say to my present waitress, "Their lives were dramatically changed that evening. They experienced a peace and joy they had never known before. By the way, have you invited Jesus Christ into *your* heart?" She hadn't. And before I left that evening, she did pray with me to receive the Lord into her life.

## Entrust the Person to the Lord

The most important thing you can do for a person you lead to the Lord is to give him to the Lord in prayer, and then trust the Lord to be with him. I often pray, "Lord, help that person to grow in you. Protect him from any enemy attack against his life. Preserve him until the day of your coming or until the day he is with you in heaven."

I take encouragement from the fact that one of the first deacons in the early church, Philip, didn't have a very long follow-up program with the Ethiopian eunuch he led to the Lord. (See Acts 8:26–39.)

Philip was led by the Holy Spirit to go to the Gaza desert and, upon seeing the Ethiopian in his chariot and hearing him read aloud from Isaiah, to approach the man. He shared the Lord with him as he traveled, baptized him when they came across a body of water, and then Philip disappeared! From what we know through studies of church history, that man returned to his home country, led the leaders of his land to the Lord, and helped to establish one of the strongest centers for Christianity in the entire region at that time. His follow-up program was one designed entirely by the Holy Spirit revealing the truth of the Scriptures to his born-anew heart. The Ethiopian—or Coptic—church is one of the oldest bodies of faith in the world.

The Scriptures say this about the sharing of God's Word: "So shall My word be that goes forth from My mouth: / It shall not return to Me void, / But it shall accomplish what I please, / And it shall prosper in the thing for which I sent it" (Isaiah 55:11). That's not only true of the Word of the Lord spoken as a part of active soul winning. That's true of any Word of the Lord spoken in the life of any believer, no matter how young he is in Christ.

Trust God to be true to His own Word. Trust God to accomplish in a person's life what He pleases.

# READY . . . SET . . . GO!

There's nothing I'd rather do than tell a person about Jesus and lead him to the Lord. I'll readily give up a meal, sleep, or a social activity if there's an opportunity to share the gospel with someone.

Leading a person to receive Jesus Christ is the greatest "high" I know—the greatest adventure, the greatest joy, the greatest satisfaction in life.

## No Plain Vanilla

A friend of mine named Charles once said to me over dinner, "I'm tired of plain vanilla Christianity."

We were both in Washington, D.C. on business and had a good dinner together sharing about our jobs and our walks with the Lord. I prayed with Charles about his desire to see the power of God at work in a new way and assured him that the Lord would answer the desire of his heart.

As we left the restaurant, we decided to walk the few blocks back toward our hotel. As we waited to cross an intersection, Charles struck up a conversation with a man who was trying to restart his truck. It had broken down as he was making a turn and was blocking part of our crosswalk. He had diagnosed the problem and called his wife, who was on her way with a carburetor part he needed. We waited with him and began to share with him about the Lord Jesus.

"The Lord must have put you in our way tonight so we could tell you about Him," we said. "Both of us have received Jesus Christ into our lives and it's the most encouraging thing that's ever happened to us. We no longer have to struggle with guilt over the things we know we have done wrong. We have a peace and joy in our lives that can't be matched. Would you like to receive the Lord into your life tonight?"

The man said yes, and we were praying with him as his wife drove up with the needed part. Their teenage daughter was in the car with her. While the man began to repair his car, we shared with his wife, "We've got great news for you! Your husband just received the Lord Jesus into his life. You need to do that, too, don't you?"

She said yes, as did the teenage daughter. Within a matter of ten or fifteen minutes from the time we came to that intersection, we were standing under the streetlight, our hands joined with those of this family in a circle of prayer. We prayed that their entire family would come to be united in Christ!

We continued toward our hotel and encountered a barefoot man, reeling under the influence of liquor and drugs. His jaw had been broken, and he was muttering unintelligible syllables. Finally, we made out his demand for a cigarette. I thought of what Peter said to the blind man at the Beautiful Gate, "Silver and gold have I none; but such as I have give I thee" (Acts 3:6). Neither Charles nor I had a cigarette to give, and the third time the man asked, I looked him straight in the eye and declared with as much authority as I could muster, "In the name of Jesus Christ. . . ."

Before I could finish the sentence, the man began to cry out, "Oh no!" He jerked into a stunned silence, as though something had hit him. I had no doubt it was the power of God. He put out his hands to brace himself against a wall behind him, and a softness began to come over his countenance. I continued to affirm the promises of God over him:

The Lord Jesus Christ is the King of kings and the Lord of lords.

The Lord Jesus Christ is taking power and authority over the power of the enemy that has been working within you.

The Lord Jesus Christ has freed you from the torment that has plagued your life.

The Lord Jesus Christ is available to you right now and you can call upon His name.

As I spoke, he stood up and his words became clearer. He put on the shoes he had been carrying in his arms, tied the laces, and we began to walk together.

By now, I had begun reciting the Twenty-third Psalm, "The LORD is my shepherd; I shall not want. . . ." When I got to the line, "I will fear no evil," he joined in, "I will fear no evil," and kept repeating that line over and over.

"The Lord has released you," I assured him, "from the satanic stronghold that was keeping you in bondage. You can call upon His name now." The man repeated the name "Jesus" softly.

I could tell he was needing rest. We hailed a cab and took him to a nearby shelter for a night's lodging. I went into the shelter with him, and Charles stayed in the cab, explaining to the driver—a Muslim from Iran—what had happened to this man. Charles' face was radiant with joy when I returned. He had led this cab driver to the Lord. The driver said he had never seen such compassion and knew that the power of God in our lives was genuine.

"Plain vanilla?" I asked Charles.

"No way!" Not for Charles. And certainly not for the truck driver and his family, the barefoot drunk, or the Iranian cab driver.

Need a lift in your spiritual life?

Win someone to the Lord! Introduce others to the living Christ.

## The Greatest Joy You Can Know

The two most exciting experiences in human existence are to receive Jesus Christ into your life and to lead others to receive Him.

If you haven't experienced the first experience, I invite you to do so today.

If you haven't led another person to Jesus Christ, I invite you to start sharing Him with others today.

Now is the time.

Don't miss out on winning the souls God causes to cross your path today. They may never cross your path again.

## My Closing Prayer with You

Heavenly Father, thank You that You are no respecter of persons. Thank You that You have shed Your own blood to purchase our lives and that You have given us all things that pertain to life and godliness through the Lord Jesus. Thank You that You desire to move us all into a new dimension of discovering how to cooperate with You and to be instruments of righteousness in confronting people with the gospel of Jesus Christ.

Let us be among those who have an expectancy in our lives more and more each day to see others come to a saving knowledge of You. Use the words that we speak as if they are Your own words, because we are one with You through the Holy Spirit. Help us to be faithful to carry out Your purposes on the earth before Your soon return.

Thank You that You have entrusted us to be stewards of the manifold grace of God and stewards of the gospel. Thank You for enabling and empowering us in this moment to be active soul winners and to know the joy of extending Your kingdom and revealing Your glory. Lead us to those we can lead to You *today*. I pray this in the incomparable name of Jesus.

Amen!